Recalling Education

RECALLING EDUCATION

HUGH MERCER CURTLER

ISI BOOKS
Wilmington, Delaware
2001

Cataloging-in-Publication Data

Curtler, Hugh Mercer
    Recalling Education / by Hugh Mercer Curtler.—1st ed.
    —Wilmington, DE : ISI Books, 2001.

    p. cm.

    ISBN 1-882926-55-2
      1. Education—Higher—Aims and objectives.
  2. Education, Humanistic. I. Title.

LB2324 .C87 2001   00-106785
387/.01—dc21   CIP

Published in the United States by:

  ISI Books
  Post Office Box 4431
  Wilmington, DE 19807-0431
  www.isibooks.org

Manufactured in the United States of America

For my students: past, present, and future

Contents

Preface

Thomas Jefferson thought that nations should have a revolution every twenty years. I assume he meant a bloodless revolution, but one that would nonetheless scrape away some of the encrusted scales of habit and enliven the beast with new energy. In this way, the constitution of a nation resembles not only that nation's people but also those institutions its people invent to help make them more human. This most certainly includes educational institutions.

The time for a revolution in American education, and higher education in particular, is long overdue. The scales are thick and the energy is low. Educators have not taken a serious look at what they do for a long time, and as a result they stumble about and grope in the dark. John Dewey and Robert Hutchins shouted at one another in the 1930s soon after Harvard College introduced the elective system in American higher education. At the end of that decade, St. John's College, adopting a plan drawn up at the University of Chicago, tried to restore the classics to a curriculum that avoided electives altogether. But since the heyday of Dewey and Hutchins there has been little in the way of deep and probing discussion of the nature and purpose of higher education. Most of the books they and others of their ilk wrote are now out of print and gather dust on forgotten shelves. Faculty members are preoccupied with other matters, and students just want to have as much fun as they can while expending as little effort as possible.

One somewhat shrill voice to emerge in the relative silence of the last fifty years was that of Allan Bloom, whose book *The Closing of the American Mind* sold millions of copies, mostly to people who either did not read it or did not understand what they read. Bloom was determined to say what he thought was wrong with American higher education and to trace its causes back through the student unrest in the sixties to, ultimately, Nietzsche. His book was largely polemical and did not really address the question of purpose. But it caused a stir, including a variety of responses (one of which I consider in Chapter 8), and it made people think. This was in keeping with Bloom's goals, which were modest: "One cannot and should not wish for a general reform.... The hope is that the embers do not die soon."[1] But in an increasingly politicized academy, nothing much came of Bloom's analysis except howls of protest from the Left and murmurs of approval from the Right.

My goal in this book is to echo some of Bloom's concerns and to add some of my own, while at the same time making some positive suggestions which arise from a careful analysis of the nature and purpose of higher education.

This analysis does not proceed by way of an examination of countless college catalogs, because one will find in them only confusion and disorder. My approach is not that of the social scientist; it is that of the philosopher: to recall just what it is that makes higher education a unique human institution, what it is supposed to do that no other human institution can do. If we can accomplish this task, we will have uncovered the purpose of higher education, and that promises to show us the way out of our present morass.

This investigation will be revolutionary, following Jefferson's recommendation. That is, it will not necessarily be new, but it will be radically different from the vague proposals and confused plans that now fill the air. As things now stand, higher education has no carefully articulated and defensible program; it flounders for lack of purpose. The academy wanders aimlessly as administrators engage in crisis management and faculty in the humanities and social sciences fight culture wars from behind barricades of incoherent verbiage. The natural scientists look up from their narrow investigations with an amused expression, while in the background the students look on, bewildered, disenchanted, disoriented, and above all else, uninterested.

The students are the ones victimized by education's lack of purpose, as I shall argue in the following chapters. But in the end it is also our democratic system that is impoverished, for her citizens increasingly become mere *subjects,* further and further removed from a system that gradually becomes unfathomable to them. The fact is, very little happens to American college and university students between the time they matriculate and the time they graduate, despite the fact, as noted by Bloom, that "true liberal education requires that the student's whole life be radically changed by it, that which he learns [should] affect his action, tastes, his choices.... [N]o previous attachment [should] be immune to examination and hence re-evaluation."[2] The reason for this, of course, is that, with rare exceptions, higher education is no longer liberal education. It has bought into myths, which I shall examine in the second chapter, and it reflects the impatience of Americans generally with "useless" subjects. This is especially true in public higher education, where taxpayers foot the bill and demand an immediate return on their investment.

I therefore begin this book by returning to the question of purpose, and—since I am convinced that the purpose of higher education is to help young men and women become free—I spend some time exploring the concept of human freedom in its connection with both education and citizenship, properly conceived. These are "old-fashioned" ideas, to some extent, but I have tried to modify them and give them a contemporary focus. I am not advocating a return to some sort of Golden Age when all things were perfect and all young people received a true education. There was no such time. But I do think we can learn from the past and borrow what is best from it as we try to anticipate the future.

The key terms at the center of my discussion—freedom, education, and citizenship—dovetail in interesting ways, as I hope to show. In the process of exhibiting these relationships, I point to some of the more glaring mistakes that have been made in education in recent decades. The revolution I call for begins with some recommendations I shall make to remedy the present situation and redirect our attention to things that matter.

Although the essays I have formed into several chapters in this book have been revised, I wish to thank *The Intercollegiate Review* for permission to reprint "Recalling the Purpose of Higher Education," which appeared in that journal under another title, and *Modern Age* for permission to reprint "Dissenting Opinion." I also want to thank *Humanitas* for permission to reprint "Can Virtue Be Taught?" and *Forum for Honors* for permission to reprint "Citizenship in a World of Differ-

ence," which also appeared in modified form as the final
chapter of my last book, *Rediscovering Values: Coming to Terms
with Postmodernism*, published by M.E. Sharpe, Armonk, N.Y.,
and is reprinted here in modified form with permission. A
portion of the chapter "How Not to Read a Book" appeared
in *Conradiana* and is reprinted here with permission. Finally,
Chapter 6, "The Liberal Arts and the Public College," appeared in a considerably altered version in the *Midwest Review*.

I am particularly grateful to my colleague Phil Cafaro and
my former students Kevin Stroup and Theo Darby for their
willingness to carefully look over the manuscript and point
out sections that required amplification or clarification. I also
thank Shawn Hedman of the Southwest State University computer services area for his invaluable assistance, and the university itself for a paid leave of absence to finish the manuscript.
Finally, I want to thank the nice people at ISI Books, who have
been most supportive throughout this book's journey to press.
I make special mention of Jeffrey Nelson, editors Christopher
Briggs and Jeremy Beer, Brooke Haas in marketing, and Claudia
Henrie in production. Whatever its shortcomings, this book
has been much improved because of their assistance.

Chapter I

THE PURPOSE OF
HIGHER EDUCATION

"In the present aspect of the world, liberty is conceived as license, whereas genuine liberty is only the mastering of one's self.... License of desires leads only to enslavement."
—Dostoevsky

No nation on earth has ever placed before its people a richer cornucopia of delights with fewer restrictions on choice than does contemporary America. But while Americans are justifiably proud of the freedom this gives them, freedom is not reducible to the many options this abundance makes possible. A person is not free, for example, simply because he sees before himself a bewildering variety of goods and has money in his pocket; that person is truly free only if he can order that variety and make it less bewildering. In one sense, freedom increases as the number of choices increases: this is what Irving Babbitt once called "the freedom of the lunatic," since, presumably, the lunatic is one who has been overwhelmed by a wide variety of choices. But freedom also involves *informed* choice, and information together with heightened powers of discrimination actually reduce the number of choices to the few that are worthy of serious consideration. This sort of freedom is called "positive freedom," or "autonomy," to the extent that such choices are our own and are not foisted upon us by someone else. It contrasts with "negative freedom," or freedom viewed simply as the number of choices available at any moment.

In order to better understand the difference between these two kinds of human freedom, consider a simple illustration. Suppose you go to a used-car lot to buy a car. Suppose, further, that you know little or nothing about cars. There are more than a hundred cars on the lot, so on the face of it you have considerable freedom. Not only can you select from among those one hundred cars, but you can also leave and go to other lots where there are more cars. My claim here is that, in this case, the freedom you have to choose the car you want is important, but limited: the fact that you are ignorant about cars restricts your freedom to choose the right car, or the car that will most suit your needs. You may get lucky (chances are at least one in a hundred), but it is more likely that you will get a car for all the wrong reasons—it looks great, your friend has one like it, or the salesman sells you the car that will garner him the largest commission. In any event, your ignorance in this case clearly limits your freedom. Increased knowledge about cars, about persuasive advertising, about the pressures that operate on salesmen forcing them to resort to trickery, together with an ability to think on your feet and recognize bloat and rhetoric for what it is, will increase your freedom and the probability that you will choose the right car. The freedom to choose one out of the hundred (or more) cars is negative freedom; the freedom to choose the right car, based on your ability to use your mind, is positive freedom (albeit, in this pedestrian example, a rather mundane use of that freedom). Ironically, negative freedom is a function of many choices; positive freedom may reduce all choices to one or very few.

As can be seen from this simple illustration, positive freedom, unlike negative freedom, is not given at birth. It must be achieved through effort, increased understanding, and the ability to use one's intellectual powers. If this is so in such a simple case as the purchase of an automobile, how much more so must it be when it comes to vital choices? Making the right choice requires more than merely the absence of restraints; it requires knowledge and the ability to think. And while negative freedom is protected in our society by a variety of institutions, positive freedom is the responsibility of schools and academies alone.

Unfortunately, our secondary schools have long shown little interest in positive freedom, thanks in large measure to John Dewey's bankrupt ideas of "growth" and "exploration," ideas that have captivated primary and secondary school education for the past sixty years. It has, therefore, devolved to the colleges and universities to help young people in our society become self-determined, to gain control of their own minds and make informed choices. For a variety of reasons, however, the academy has largely ignored this responsibility.

In this chapter, I will consider reasons why this has occurred. To do this, I shall need to begin with a consideration of the nature of higher education and then turn to some of the factors that have come between institutions of higher education and their purpose. In the end, I shall recommend several specific steps to restore a sense of purpose to the academy.

"Education," from the Latin, literally means "to draw forth." We find this enlightening, however, only if we know what it is that is being drawn forth. As traditionally conceived, education draws forth the distinctly *human* potential that lies within every person. This means that while educators should not ignore the particular individuals they deal with, they should concern themselves primarily with what people have in common and what makes humans unique as a species.

According to Aristotle, to say that educators should try to draw forth our "common human potential" is to say that educators are to be concerned with virtue (*arete*); in humans this requires, once character has been formed, that reason be developed in order to make self-directed activity possible. That is to say, human potential is realized to the extent that the formulation of and adherence to a person's own reasonable plans or objectives arise out of good character.

Aristotle's concern with reason is not a narrow concern, as is commonly charged: we are speaking of the *whole person* when we speak of his "rational animal," and "reason" is not merely "intelligence" or "learning" any more than education is mere schooling. Scott Buchanan noted this when he said, "Our emotions are under the reason and so are other things like perception.... [I]f you are educating anybody, the channel, the medium through which you do this, will be rational."[1] The result, if it is achieved successfully, will be autonomy, or what Brand Blanshard once called "reasonableness." He described it as follows:

> By reasonableness I do not mean intelligence, though that may be a great help. Attila, Torquemada, and Stalin were highly intelligent men, but they were not reasonable men. Nor is a reasonable man necessarily a learned man, for learning may be present without even ordinary common sense. No; the reasonableness of which I am speaking is a settled disposition to guide one's belief and conduct by the evidence. It is a bent of the will to order one's thought by the relevant facts, to order one's practice in the light of the values involved, to make reflective judgment the compass of one's belief and action.[2]

The goal of achieving reasonableness has traditionally been

bound up with the liberal arts. Aristotle coined the term "art," which involves "knowledge of universals" applied by "practical reason" to concrete problems of the *polis*, or civic community. Western tradition, for the most part, has followed this usage.

The original seven liberal arts formulated during the Middle Ages comprised the trivium of grammar, logic, and rhetoric, combined with the quadrivium of arithmetic, geometry, astronomy, and music. These seven arts have proliferated, and now the liberal arts include all those subjects within the humanities, social sciences, and natural sciences that free the mind from enslavement to inclination, habit, and passion through the application of principles and deeper understanding. This is the current interpretation of what Aristotle meant when he characterized the liberal arts as "knowledge of universals" applied by "practical reason."

We should recall that, despite their practical application, the liberal arts are not "techniques." They do not focus on "know-how," as does so much of what is currently taught in our colleges and universities. The liberal arts liberate the human mind by enabling it to make informed choices and, through a knowledge of theory and principles, to understand why such choices must be made.

To the extent that a reasonable person is autonomous, he will be able to resist hucksterism, coercion, and intimidation; recognize exaggeration and prevarication; determine what is fact and what is not; and distinguish between an opinion that is supported by evidence and argument and one that merely feels comfortable. Note once again that autonomy is an acquired trait, not something we are born with.

It is important to distinguish the concept of autonomy defended here from the highly individualistic, even narcissistic, misconception advanced in the last fifty years by pop psychologists and their intellectual fathers, Abraham Maslow, Carl Jung, Erich Fromm, Rollo May, and (especially) Carl Rogers. The traditional concept of autonomy traces its roots back through Kant and Rousseau to the theistic concept of positive freedom, which centers around the notion of doing the right thing. The popular view, as advanced by those Paul Vitz calls "selfist theorists," is thoroughly relativistic and rules out all normative dimensions of human experience. From this perspective, to be autonomous is to "do your own thing," and if your thing happens to be lynching your black neighbor, so be it. (As Vitz has noted in this regard, "...[B]oth black and white racism are perfectly consistent with self-theory.")[3] This popular conception of autonomy rests on the faulty notion that humans are basically good and that evil comes from somewhere else—usually the family or society in general. The weight of current psychological theory, fortunately, calls this view into question; Donald Campbell, for one, goes so far as to say that there is "social functionality and psychological validity to the concepts of sin and temptation and of original sin due to human carnal, animal nature."[4] It is more accurate to say that humans are neither good nor bad; we are an odd mix of both, which is something we should have learned from reading Shakespeare, Dostoevsky, and Freud.

But what passes for educational theory these days is a thin soup containing a few crumbs collected from under the tables of these popularizers. Thus do we hear a great deal about "encouraging self-esteem," "promoting self-actualization," and "realizing one's own true potential," with no regard whatever for the question of what one's potential might happen to be or whether one is deserving of high self-esteem. As Vitz has pointed out, there seems to be little or no relation between high self-esteem and true human accomplishment,[5] and children, once again, are neither inherently good nor bad; they are both.

Nevertheless, the pop psychologists' sort of theoretical soup is swallowed with great delight in most schools of education and is especially pervasive at the primary and secondary levels, where teachers are admonished not to be "judgmental," and activities such as "values clarification" are all the rage. Thus, it is important to make clear that the autonomy that belongs at the center of classical educational theory bears little or no resemblance to that which is bandied about by popularizers and bogus educational "theorists."

A democratic society must presume that its citizens are capable of reasonable actions. By way of developing that capacity, therefore, it becomes the responsibility of certain institutions in a democratic society to prepare young minds for citizenship—that is, reasonable action in the political sphere. This is where the goal of higher education and the requirements of a free society overlap. Confusion of purpose within the academy affects all members of a free society, and the liberal arts must therefore be defended against those who would reduce education to child care or vocational training (or both) and the academies to waystations that provide the latest soporifics to a community in constant agitation. But it would seem this is precisely what has occurred. Why is this? What has gone wrong?

To answer these questions, we need to separate those factors that operate within the walls of the academy from those that operate from without. Regarding the latter, we need only mention briefly that the single, clear role of the academy in our society has become confused as a result, in part at least, of the increasing ineffectiveness of the family and churches as viable social institutions. As a consequence of this degeneration, our schools are now expected to solve every problem, to be all things to all people, and this exacts promises from the schools that they cannot possibly hope to deliver.

But even if the family and our churches were healthy, confusion abounds within the walls of academe on the part of those who should be clearest about what it is they do, and it is to this internal confusion that we shall now turn. There appear to be three major causes of the confusion of purpose within higher education: (1) over-administration; (2) over-specialization; and (3) diminished concern with education *per se*.

Members of college and university faculties have probably always complained about the number of administrators, and they probably always will. In recent times, however, the situation has taken an alarming turn. Institutions of higher learning in America are currently overrun with people whose role is not central to the purpose of education but who, nonetheless, seek to legitimize their positions within the academy by carving out territory and fortifying it with a barricade of jargon. This includes droves of minor administrators and so-called "non-teaching faculty" in areas such as athletics, student affairs, housing, counseling, employment services, drug rehabilitation, affirmative action, minority recruiting, and "learning resources" (read: "remedial learning"). This is the direct result of the social demands placed upon the academy because of the collapse of other viable social institutions. What we need to note here is simply that the strain placed on scarce resources and the limited energies of those who take their task seriously must necessarily weaken and fractionalize the central purpose of education.

Recent data regarding this phenomenon are astonishing. In an article in *The Chronicle of Higher Education,* a report by the U.S. Equal Opportunity Commission indicated that between 1975 and 1985 the increase in full-time faculty in this country was 5.9 percent. During that same period, the increase in the number of administrators was 17.9 percent and the increase in the number of "other professionals," presumably support personnel and non-teaching faculty, was 61.1 percent.[6]

Someone once said that the reason the railroads are in trouble in this country is because they have forgotten that their business is to move passengers rather than trains. The situation is quite similar among institutions of higher learning: running the institution, including introducing new programs and hiring functionaries whose roles are obscure, has become an end in itself. This phenomenon is little more than the most recent consequence of what Jacques Ellul dubbed "the technological imperative," or the inversion of the proper relationship between means and ends. Put simply, the technological imperative dictates that the means to given ends become ends themselves—and attention to ends, why it is that something is being done, disappears. The key word in a technological society is "efficiency." Ellul made the point rather vividly in 1954:

> Technical progress today is no longer conditioned by anything other than its own calculus of efficiency. The search is no longer personal, experimental, workmanlike; it is abstract,

mathematical, and industrial. This does not mean that the individual no longer participates. On the contrary, progress is made only after innumerable individual experiments. But the individual participates only to the degree that he is subordinate to the search for efficiency, to the degree that he resists all the currents today considered secondary, such as aesthetics, ethics, fantasy. Insofar as the individual represents this abstract tendency, he is permitted to participate in technical creation, which is increasingly independent of him and increasingly linked to its own mathematical law.[7]

At the time Ellul was writing his book, the technological imperative was already operating in the realm of education, as rapidly evolving "teachers' colleges" increasingly offered curricula focused almost exclusively on considerations of method, with no concern for goals. The current problem is not new; it is simply getting worse.

Over-specialization, the second factor mentioned above, is also not new, and it is also getting worse. A phenomenon born and nurtured within the academy itself, over-specialization has made it increasingly difficult for members of college and university faculties to share any sense of common purpose. As a result, it is virtually impossible to get faculty volunteers to teach basic "general education" courses, or to deal in a systematic way with questions of how to order and integrate the curriculum. The sad fact is that members of college and university faculties are not prepared to discuss these issues as professionals. Often they cannot. The resulting fragmentation of knowledge further widens the gap between the ideal of liberal education and what currently passes for education within the academy.

The problems associated with over-specialization may go back as far as late in the nineteenth century, when Harvard College introduced the elective curriculum. The elective curriculum itself, however, was the product of over-specialization, the inevitable outcome of the granting of Ph.D.'s in narrow fields that produced specialists whose main objective was to turn out more specialists. Michael Polanyi noted the problem in the sciences in 1957 when he wrote:

> The organization of scientific progress is determined, in the first place, by the fact that modern science is so vast that any single person can properly understand only a small fraction of it. The Royal Society has eight sub-committees for the election of Fellows, each of which has a separate field of research allotted to it. One of these fields, for example, is mathematics; but individual mathematicians are further specialized and are competent to deal only with a small part of mathematics. It is a rare mathematician—we are told—who fully understands more than half a dozen out of fifty papers presented to a mathematical congress.... Adding to this evidence my own experience in chemistry and physics, it seems to me that the situation may be similar for all the major scientific provinces, so that any single scientist may be competent to judge at first hand only about one hundredth of the total current output of science.[8]

If we consider that this comment was made more than forty years ago, we can compound the problem in the sciences and then apply it, *pari passu,* to the social sciences and humanities, though the problem is less pronounced outside the natural sciences, where at least lip service is paid to interdisciplinary pursuits. One need only look closely at any department of philosophy or English at a major university, however, to see the same sort of narrow specialization that concerned Polanyi.

From this vantage point, we need not look far to see why a great many faculty members are unable to find common ground on which to discuss the critical issue of "general education" with their colleagues. Time has led to the promotion of specialized disciplines, the expansion of major requirements, and an ongoing battle to increase the numbers of major students within departments. None of these concerns has anything to do with education *per se,* and yet they are of central importance to many who set the academic tone. Allan Bloom was surely right when he pointed out the irony that the "great universities which can split the atom, find cures for the most dreaded diseases, conduct surveys of whole populations, and produce dictionaries of lost languages...cannot generate a modest program of general education for undergraduate students. This is a parable for our times."[9]

The tendency to focus attention on academic disciplines is closely related to the last item on our list of concerns, and may stem from the same deeper causes. It is the diminishing concern among members of college and university faculties over matters that do not affect them directly.[10] What is of concern are such things as job security, protecting territory, and promoting "diversity."

The fact that members of university faculties are on average older than they were in the past is a matter of historical accident. However, taken together with the consideration that many institutions of higher education are involved in a struggle to survive, and that jobs are difficult to find (and hold on to), the fact that there are more older faculty members now than ever before—and that these people have a lock on tenure positions—partly explains the current worries over job security among younger, untenured faculty, many of whom work as adjuncts, struggling to find a toehold in higher education. These worries, in turn, partly explain the lack of energy and attention to the things that should matter most to students. Some years ago, Gabriel Marcel warned us that "as soon as a preoccupation with security begins to dominate human life, the scope of human life itself tends to be diminished. Life, as it were, tends to shrink back on itself, to wither."[11] The tendency of interests to become narrow and of long-range concerns to shorten, of "life shrinking back on itself," surfaces everywhere in the academy as efforts to protect territory, or areas of special interest and concern to faculty members themselves, become paramount concerns. Evidence of this is not hard to come by.

One of the more interesting examples occurs in a recent Carnegie Foundation study of the preparedness of students entering college. The study showed that members of diverse academic areas agreed that students generally were "seriously unprepared" for college. This assessment was confirmed by faculty members in virtually every academic department—except those in education departments, which is to say those departments that are turning out the teachers of these students. Three-quarters of the college professors surveyed indicated that students with whom they have "close contact" are seriously unprepared in basic skills. The number of professors agreeing with this claim was as high as 80 percent (in mathematics), while only 50 percent of professors in education agreed. This is clear evidence of a group with a jaundiced perspective protecting its territory, and it raises profound questions about the willingness of these people to even consider issues of first importance to their students.[12]

To make matters worse, the academy has recently given birth to cadres of true believers whose goal is to promote "cultural diversity" in the name of social justice. These people are convinced that the liberal arts tradition, as they understand it, is reeking with the stench of sexism, racism, and class privilege. Not only do they refuse to defend that tradition, they attack it at every turn. I shall have more to say about this movement in subsequent chapters.[13]

In the face of this agitation and preoccupation with matters of secondary importance, the liberal arts struggle to find a place at the table. If there were other viable suggestions about what to place at the core of higher education, the problem would not be as serious as it is. But none seems forthcoming, and none will as long as the issue of purpose is never raised.

Clearly, the gap between the ideal of liberal education in a democratic society and the reality we see today grows ever wider. The question is what, if anything, can be done about it? I shall suggest a number of steps at this point that would help to remedy the situation. In the final chapter, I shall elaborate and add several more. In making these suggestions, I shall invoke a rather simple principle: the academy must once again focus attention on the ideal of liberal education as the attainment of positive human freedom.

With this in mind, and recalling the three major causes of our current malaise—over-specialization, over-administration, and diminished concern with the goals and purpose of education—we can begin by noting that the number and function of nonteaching faculty and administrators ought to be re-evaluated with a focus on the central purpose of higher education. That purpose, I have argued, is to empower young people to achieve individual autonomy. Furthermore, this must be accomplished in a brief period of time. Undergraduates will spend fewer than 2,000 clock hours in class over a four-year period—about the same amount of time they will spend on a job in their *first year* after graduation.

The major effort to realize the purpose of a liberal education occurs, if it occurs at all, in the classroom. Accordingly, academic programs must not be allowed to suffer in order to accommodate the latest trends in education or to hire personnel whose place in the academy is not even remotely connected with liberal education. This is not to say that institutions of higher learning ought to be insensitive to vital concerns, such as social justice or the need of their students to find employment after graduation. It is also not to say that cultural diversity is an unimportant factor in establishing an atmosphere in which students will grow intellectually. Nor is it to say that those within the academy should not continue to rethink the question of purpose and make changes when those changes will accommodate the students' real needs. It is simply to say that we must never lose sight of the fact that the most vital need of every student is to be able to use his mind. All else is secondary.

If Arnold Toynbee were writing today, he would doubtless warn us that our civilization, like those before it, is entering a "time of troubles." In this regard, the term "crisis" is heard on every hand and, overworked though it is, the term at least seems to apply to higher education. The role of preserver and transmitter of high culture, a role that the academy has played since the Middle Ages, is being seriously questioned within the academy itself as part of its apparently inexorable move toward cultural pluralism. Furthermore, as we have seen, the academy suffers from confusion of purpose, coupled with a disturbing reluctance on the part of those responsible for education to raise the question of purpose in the first place.

The times are out of joint: the academy is floundering in the midst of a turbulent society that makes demands upon it that have nothing whatever to do with its central educational role. It is essential, therefore, to rethink the question of purpose and regain a clear focus. My suggestion is that we must begin by recognizing, minimally, that a democratic society has more real need for reasonable citizens than it does for accountants, engineers, schoolteachers, or Ph.D.'s. If the academy is to accomplish anything worthwhile in the years to come, all other demands that have been placed upon it must stand and wait their turn.

Chapter II

DEBUNKING SOME MYTHS

"How difficult it is to establish liberty solidly among people who have lost the practice of it, and even the correct notion of it!"—Tocqueville

We are in large measure a product of the stories we tell about ourselves. This theme has become quite popular among advocates of what is derisively called "political correctness." They recognize that the words we use to describe women and minorities can fix these persons in a particular cultural framework. Accordingly, when women are called "girls," black males are called "boys," or entire groups of people are called "primitive," we perpetuate myths about these groups of people that tighten the grip of those who would maintain the "inferiority" of these people. As a result, these groups are disenfranchised and lose their status as moral persons.

I have no quarrel with myths, as a general rule, and would insist that cultures are built around a host of myths that provide spiritual sustenance. Myths do not sustain us, though, when they trap and ensnare the unwitting—as when they blend fiction with truth in captivating ways. We cannot always separate the elements of truth and half-truth from blatant falsehood, and this is when myths become dangerous. We become lulled into thinking we understand what is still unknown; we mistake stereotypes for universal truths and vapid generalizations for profound insight.

This is certainly true in education, where a number of myths that dictate educational policy and perpetuate deceptions have taken root. In this chapter, I note a number of popular myths about education and suggest that they are dangerously wrong-headed, despite—or because of—the fact that they contain an element of truth. Along the way, I consider some more accurate and helpful ways of looking at and talking about education.

Myth #1 holds that "education is job training." This myth wields a powerful influence in American culture generally and educational circles in particular. It was almost certainly started in the 1950s by educators attempting to persuade young pupils to stay in school instead of dropping out to go to work. The myth rests on the correlation between years in school and earning power, which does persist to a certain extent. But it winks at the possibility that this correlation is not causal. Thus the myth rests on the *post hoc* fallacy, since it is quite possible that the relationship between incomes and schooling is accidental. That is, it is quite possible that higher earning power comes to those who stay in school not because they have more schooling, but because they enjoy the privileges that make continued schooling possible—opportunities provided by social status and family priorities, for example. These privileges put a premium on schooling and open doors of opportunity to better-paying jobs after school.

But educators cannot possibly keep up with changes in the job market or the latest technical advances in the world of commerce. Nor can they possibly anticipate the change in mind-set of the students themselves once they enter the job market. Recent data show, for example, that "only one in three [employees] have held the same job for five years, and one in five are in their fourth or higher job in five years."[1] Thus, our schools are stymied when jobs are scarce and graduates cannot find decent work—a condition that is becoming increasingly familiar. The result is that growing numbers of students conclude that there is no good reason to stay in school. If the schools cannot find jobs for students, in this view, they are failing to do what they are supposed to do. The element of truth here, of course, is that colleges and universities cannot ignore the fact that their students need to be employable. But the claim that jobs must be the focal point of the educational process is bogus. For, like the myths that follow, it proceeds from a flawed philosophical understanding: the very idea of "vocational education" is an oxymoron.

As I argued in the last chapter, education is about freedom: it is the systematic process of putting young people into possession of their own minds. In the true sense of the word, education is about *empowerment*, the freedom that enables persons to act in accordance with their own self-determined ends. The freedom here is "positive" freedom, or autonomy, and it is contrasted, as we have seen, with negative freedom. Positive freedom relates to the human will; negative freedom relates to action. "Will" in this context involves choice, and this is why educators should focus attention here: educated persons seek to make informed choices that will lead to effective action. Both kinds of freedom are important, but positive freedom is the domain of educators.

Each way of viewing human freedom has had its defenders over the years. Positive freedom has its roots in the Stoic notion of acceptance; it dominated Western thought throughout the Medieval period when God's freedom, considered as spontaneity arising from His omnipotence, was paradigmatic, and it was central in the thinking of the Continental Rationalists. Leibniz, for example, saw no conflict whatever between the freedom of the monads and his doctrine of pre-established harmony, though Spinoza put it best when he said that "a free man is one who lives under the guidance of reason, who is not led by fear, but who directly desires that which is good; in other words, who strives to act, to live, and to preserve his being on the basis of seeking his own true advantage."[2]

This definition can best be understood if we focus on the term "act," which is distinguished from "passion" in that the latter includes those activities whose source is "outside" the agent, while the former are those activities whose source is "within" the agent. To avoid metaphors, it might better be said that action is that which occurs in accordance with rules that are self-imposed, whereas passion does not. In this sense, freedom will result from "self-determination," which is often pitted against the passions and strong feelings that are clearly "inner" (they are certainly ours) but are nonetheless likely to lead us away from our best interest (our "own true advantage"). A free man or woman is one who can resist forces that act counter to his or her long-range self-interest, whether these forces be within or without.

"Self" in this context means the rational self, and self-imposed action is action that follows from intelligent, deliberate choice. Passion, then, includes those activities that result from coercion by another person or persons or by greed, lust, rage, excessive desire for pleasure, and so on. The key to the difference between action and passion is the proper use of reason. Passion results from those nondecisions that occur out of ignorance or the impotence of reason. But when we *act* we are in control of ourselves, like Plato's charioteer in the *Phaedrus*. To be sure, control of one's will by reason is a matter of degree, but Hume was wrong to insist that reason "is and ought to be a slave of the passions." We can become self-determined when we decide to act counter to passion and strong emotion—as when we enter a dark room after convincing ourselves that the noise we heard was only the cat. Action, in Spinoza's sense of that term, is the essential ingredient of positive, as opposed to negative, freedom.

Positive freedom was translated into "moral freedom" by Rousseau in his *Social Contract*, and it became the focus for Kant in developing the notion of autonomy in his ethical theory. There are elements of the concept of positive freedom in John Locke's discussion of paternalism in his *Second Treatise on Civil Government,* but Locke's concern for human rights moved him in the direction of negative freedom, following Thomas Hobbes, and this notion has come to dominate English and American thinking about freedom generally. Negative freedom, or "liberty," had its most eloquent defense in John Stuart Mill's essay by that name.

Isaiah Berlin is one of the few contemporary thinkers to pay much attention to what he called "positive liberty," but he followed Mill in his preference for "negative liberty," or the liberty of the citizen struggling against encroachment by the political state. Although many contemporary ethical theorists have continued to concern themselves with positive freedom, in the guise of autonomy, the notion of positive freedom has been almost totally displaced since the Enlightenment by a concern for negative freedom in connection with human rights. "Freedom" has come increasingly to mean "freedom-to-do" in the face of factors that would encroach and enslave. Indeed, this reduction of freedom to negative liberty led Irving Babbitt to exclaim that "what seems to me to be driving our whole civilization toward the abyss at present is a one-sided conception of liberty, a conception that is purely centrifugal, that would get rid of all outer control and then evade or deny openly the need of achieving inner control."[3]

Be that as it may, both concepts have impressive pedigrees and have been an important part of our Western intellectual heritage. But with the possible exception of R. S. Peters in his book *Ethics and Education*, no one has attempted to link educational theory directly to a clearly conceived defense of positive freedom—and this despite the fact that the education of human beings has always had as its proper focus the achievement of autonomy, or self-determination. This focus is implicit in the thinking of the best twentieth-century educational theorists, such as Robert Hutchins, Scott Buchanan, Mortimer Adler, and Mark Van Doren. But it needs to be made explicit, especially now, when educational theory lacks focus.

We need to remind ourselves that the *liberal* arts are those intellectual disciplines that free the human mind from enslavement to habit, excessive emotion, impulse, ignorance, and the undue influence of others. They help us to make informed choices, including moral choices, based on adequate knowledge. In the end, the liberal arts help people achieve autonomy, positive freedom, or self-determination—all different names for the same thing.

We are, however, a long way from attaining that ideal, and our sense of it becomes weaker as the days pass and the din around us becomes louder. Compounding that difficulty is the cluster of myths that deludes us into thinking we know what we are about when, in fact, we do not. I have noted the most debilitating myth—education-as-job-training—but let me turn to some of the others that have become commonplace. Two of them can be taken together.

Myth #2 states that "education is schooling," while Myth #3 insists that "education is information." The former glosses over the fact that no *amount* of schooling will guarantee that a person is educated. If this were not so, only those with "terminal degrees" could be considered well-educated, and we know this to be false. Our world is full of well-schooled people who are clearly miseducated, and there are rare but significant examples of people with no formal schooling who are remarkably well educated. Eric Hoffer was a prime example.

What is important is not how much time a person has spent in school, but what the person did while there. There may be no truth to this myth whatever, though we would hope that by sending our young to school they would become educated. In some cases they do, in others they do not. At times it almost seems accidental.

We encounter Myth #3 at every turn; we read and hear daily that people need to be "educated" about AIDS, sex, drugs, health reform, or whatever. What we mean is that they need to be *informed* about these things. For while it is certainly true to say that information is a necessary condition of education, information is not sufficient. Once again we have uncovered a half-truth.

To be sure, education requires information, but more importantly, it requires that a person be able to *process* that information, to make informed choices and wise decisions. We scramble to place our young on the "information super-highway," without considering whether they can find their way. Information does us no good unless we can discriminate between important information and useless information. As John Henry Newman pointed out, "Education consists not only in the passive reception into the mind of a number of ideas hitherto unknown to it, but in the mind's energetic and simultaneous action upon and towards and among those new ideas."[4] To borrow a distinction from Irving Babbitt, an educated person must be able to assimilate knowledge, not merely to accumulate it. This fact is overlooked and becomes more compelling as the amount of information threatens to overwhelm us.

As we saw in the previous chapter, the simplest examples of informed choice—even a decision about which car to buy—allow us to see how an education empowers us to actively participate in the decision-making process, to assimilate information, and to make decisions of our own. Empowered, autonomous persons can distinguish between the true and the false, the reasonable and the unreasonable, appearance and reality, the important and the unimportant. They can detect intellectual sleight-of-hand and successfully resist the most subtle attempt at coercion, even in its cleverest disguise.

Thus, we can easily translate the abstract notion of "autonomy" into countless daily examples of responsible, thoughtful action that incorporate information, but require careful scrutiny and analysis of that information. Education may or may not require schooling, but it certainly requires the ability to process information. People are not necessarily well educated because they win big money on "Jeopardy", or because they did time in the Ivy League. One is an educated person only if one's mind is one's own. As Mark Van Doren noted, "There is no companion comparable to a mind that can be used; none more trustworthy or agreeable. It can do things nothing else can do.... It arms us against thugs who care only what we think, not how. It assists us through the jungle of opinion where things only seem to exist, where beliefs only seem to be sufficient, and where conventions only seem to compel."[5]

Myth #4 is of recent origin, but the number of the devoted chanting the mantra grows daily. This myth states that "education is enculturation," and it questions the possibility of developing *human* potential because of a preoccupation with cultural differences.

It would be fatuous to deny the heterogeneity among the cultural groups that make up what is loosely called the American "melting pot." But critics of the melting pot, acting as if this had been an original criticism, insist that we must now "privilege" difference. I would argue that, to the contrary, our differences are accidental and do not take precedence over our basic similarities as human beings. Indeed, they cannot, or education is an exercise in futility. We would be well advised to recall that culture is, in the words of Matthew Arnold, "a pursuit of our total perfection by means of getting to know on all matters that most concern us, the best that has been thought and said in the world."[6]

It is quite possible that those who argue back and forth on this issue—on either side—are guilty of bifurcation: people are totally alike or they are totally different. What goes ignored is the fact that persons are different by virtue of their gender, cultural, or subcultural particularity, but they are the same by virtue of the fact that they are all human. To paraphrase Giambattista Vico, different people may speak different languages, but they all use language. That fact is central, but is for some reason ignored.

Of related interest is another of the eddies that swirls about in these discussions, one that would have us reject the notion, among other things, that humans are in any way unique, which I imply when I insist not only that humans are essentially alike, but that educators must focus attention on human autonomy. Many of the defenders of this view, taking their cue from deep ecology, are of the opinion that humans are in no fundamental way different from other animals. Despite the fact that I am somewhat sympathetic with this view, I think it is mistaken and that it takes us in the wrong direction.

The recent determination to deny uniqueness to humans rests upon the well-meaning desire to thwart the sometimes arrogant claims that non-human animals do not matter. But the denial of human uniqueness reaches absurd heights when it argues for animal "rights" on the grounds, typically, that non-human animals have *interests* no less than human animals do. This is a spurious argument and, moreover, one that weakens the concept of rights to the point where it becomes useless.

The argument of that most romantic of scientific popularizers, Carl Sagan, is interesting in this context. In his final book, Sagan runs through the many qualities proposed throughout the years as distinctive human qualities—such things as reason, conscience, sense of humor, and the like—to show that other animals exhibit these same qualities. That fact, together with the fact that human DNA is nearly identical to that of the chimpanzee, allows him to insist that humans can make no legitimate claims to uniqueness whatever.[7]

What Sagan fails to consider in his list of qualities, however, is precisely the capacity humans have to obey self-imposed rules and laws: autonomy. And it is this capacity, whether we ever choose to realize it, that makes humans unique and even "superior," in the sense that we have the capacity to recognize our duty to respect all life and diminish suffering whenever possible. This is a capacity that should not make us smug; on the contrary, it is one that should make us humble, because it places on our shoulders a responsibility that, as far as we know, is not shared by any other creature: namely, the responsibility to respect others.

I place "superior" in scare-quotes because I recognize that while our uniqueness generates both rights and responsibilities that are not shared with other animals, it also places the atrocities humans have committed against one another, against other animals, and even against our environment, in a glaring light—precisely because we should have known better. To be sure, in this regard humans are inferior to other animals. But having said this, we must not shrink from the fact that the human capacity for autonomy is something other animals do not have. And it is precisely this capacity that education must focus upon. I do not think we can teach "virtue," as I shall argue in Chapter 7, but I would insist that we can help develop the capacities students have to act ethically by enabling them to use their minds, by making them more self-determined and more intelligent.

The point of this apparent digression is that humans, despite their differences from one another, are similar in their capacity to make moral choices—as R. S. Peters put it, to ask, "Why should I be ethical?"—and are different from all the other animals for the same reason. Humans have the capacity to achieve positive freedom. But this is a capacity that can be developed only through education, properly conceived.

If we recall the purpose of higher education, we note that the concept incorporates skills that are basic to every person. No matter who the student might be, the proper concern of educators must always be with that person as a potential agent, that is, as a person who wants to become free. The skills that make autonomy possible are fundamental skills that are required by anyone in the modern world, regardless of that person's gender or cultural background. We may acknowledge that non-Western cultures have been too long ignored, as have minority literature, art, and history, and correcting this oversight may well affect both the manner and matter of what is taught. But it is not necessary to "privilege" difference.

In fact, the education-as-enculturation myth is a variation on the education-as-information myth. It insists that blacks, for example, will be properly educated if and only if they are informed about who they are and what is unique about their history. Presumably this can only be done by black teachers, even if—as some maintain—the information is historically inaccurate. This view not only erases the distinction between truth and fiction, but it is contradictory: it assumes that blacks (or women and other minorities) will suffer irreparable damage if subjected to another cultural perspective, while maintaining at the same time that awareness of multiple cultures is fundamental to education! It also insists, wrongly, that individual freedom and self-worth are only possible by means of group identity and group loyalty. This is a mistake of the first order, since true individuality can be achieved only through autonomy, through the possession of one's own mind. To make self-worth a function of commitment to a group (any group) can in fact rob us of our identity, since we cannot be sure that our decisions are our own. Indeed, according to Jacob Burckhardt, Western man achieved his characteristic individuality only *after* breaking with guilds and political groups with whom he identified in the Middle Ages. Before that, as Burckhardt noted, "man was conscious of himself only as a member of a race, people, party, family, or corporation—only through some general category."[8] The notion that a person can achieve a sense of self-worth only by identifying with a group is not only bad psychology, it is historically blind.

Among other things, those who adopt this myth assume, if they do not insist, that education is ideological. I shall pursue this topic further in Chapter 3. Here I shall only note in passing that education need not be ideological if teaching is dialectical and not doctrinal. I would say, further, that any subject can be taught by anyone knowledgeable about the subject matter, and if it is taught well it will not be ideological. Teaching can be damaging only if a particular perspective is presented as the only possible perspective. But if a perspective is presented as simply one point of view and the goal is to enable the student to think, that is, to arrive at his or her own perspective, content need not degenerate into doctrine, and pedagogy need not become proselytizing. The issue is not who does the teaching, but how it is done.

Simply because a person is informed about what is going on, we cannot assume that that person has gained any real understanding. Just because a point is stressed and repeated, one cannot assume that any real thought has occurred. Information in and of itself, as I have said above, is not sufficient to free the human mind. That mind must be able to assimilate that information: one must be able to think.

There remains one final myth, Myth #5, one born of our economic system and our penchant for analogies based on the business world. This is the myth that "education is a marketplace" and that students are "consumers" who pay for a "product" and should therefore be guaranteed their money back if not entirely satisfied. Recently, the courts have been forced to wrestle with this fiction, but it distorts the major objectives of education and should therefore concern all who hope to help students take possession of their own minds. To the extent that teachers adopt this myth, they simply become merchants hawking their goods in the town square, where emphasis is on eye appeal, competition is the primary motivator, and customer satisfaction is the measure of success. Those who succumb to this myth ruin their students' minds by serving them a thin gruel that can be swallowed whole, warms the tummy, and leaves a pleasant taste in the mouth, but provides no real nutrition.

Students *are* paying for something, and herein lies the element of truth in this myth. But this "something" is not a "product" and students are not, strictly speaking, consumers. They are uneducated persons who desperately need to learn how to use their minds—whether they know that or not. And their teachers fail them to the extent that they fail to provide them with a coherent course of study that will prepare them for an uncertain future. To view students as consumers is to cater to their "needs," which is to say their desires—desires that are almost always short-term, uninformed, and fickle. How can they be otherwise?

Students may know what they want, but it is not clear that they know what they need. When Charles Eliot introduced the elective system at Harvard early in the last century, he noted that teachers are not omniscient and therefore should not determine for their students what courses to take. To be sure, members of faculties are not all-knowing, but they know more than their students. If they do not, they should—or their students are wasting their time and money.

Schools are more like hospitals than marketplaces, though neither analogy is quite apt, since schools are *sui generis*. They do what no other social institution does: they educate (or they should). Whatever the failings of contemporary faculty, do we really want to argue that students who have only begun to achieve freedom are in a better position to know what a well-educated person needs to succeed in a confusing world than their teachers, who have the benefit of years and have learned, one would hope, where the traps and pitfalls lie? An affirmative response to this question implies that those who teach have no responsibility to their students. After all, if students are consumers they should simply be given what they demand. If what they are sold does them no good, so be it: from the "seller's" point of view, *caveat emptor.* Such a view is not only irresponsible, it is mean.

The schools will, eventually, confer diplomas and degrees on their students, and the ceremony (which we call "commencement" without giving much thought to what that might mean) symbolizes the certification by the faculty that the graduates are ready to go on to the next stage of schooling or into the "real" world. This does not simply mean that they are competent chemists, accountants, or teachers of history. Ideally, it means that they are closer to positive freedom than they were four years previously.

The fact that the commencement exercise has become mere ceremony should not blind us to its particular significance. Graduates are now entering a new stage in the ongoing process of becoming free persons. If those in our institutions of education are to certify this, they must not lose sight of what it is that makes higher education different from the host of other public and private institutions in modern society. They must learn to mistrust the half-truths about education that engender confusion. Succumbing to myths makes us lose sight of what is central to education and why it is a unique process.

Indeed, each of these myths in its own way "captures the minds" of those who are taken in by them. It is precisely this sort of captivity that is anathema to education, properly conceived. The freedom that education promotes is the student's freedom to use his or her own mind, which necessitates freedom from the myths and fictions that ensnare and render powerless.

Chapter III

EDUCATION
OR INDOCTRINATION?

"Paradoxically enough a teacher must both be an authority and teach in such a way that pupils become capable of showing him where he is wrong."
—R. S. Peters

I have claimed that the goal of education is autonomy, "putting young men and women into possession of their own minds." The objective of the present chapter is to clarify and defend this claim.

The term "autonomy" comes from two Greek words for "self" and "law," and Kant used the term in its strictest possible meaning: persons differ from things (and other animals), according to Kant, because they have the capacity to follow laws of their own making. Everything else in nature obeys the laws of physics or animal impulse. Only persons can thwart those laws, to an extent, and "act for the sake of duty." It is this sense of autonomy that lies at the heart of education. Young people are not free at birth; they become free only after they have

been properly educated. Thus viewed, education is the process whereby rational agents achieve autonomy and are thereby
empowered to decide and act for themselves.

The concept of autonomy has come under attack recently
by feminist philosophers like Carol Gilligan, who regards the
notion as excessively "masculine."[1] Aside from the fact that this
is a sexist claim, it is also most certainly false. Men are not the
only persons who desire to become empowered: all persons
desire it (or they should), since it is the essence of what it
means to be human. (It should be noted in passing that "empowerment" as I use it here does not exclude the ethics of
care: self-determined activity is perfectly consistent with a concern for others.) But how can young persons achieve empowerment through "higher" education? It will not do to simply
throw them into an elective system without direction, even if
that's what they think they want. As Locke astutely warned, it
is a serious mistake to "turn [a person] loose to an unrestrained
liberty before he has reason to guide him," since that is simply
to "thrust him out amongst brutes and abandon him to a state
as wretched and as much beneath that of a man as theirs."[2]

As I have insisted throughout this book, students who are
given a wide variety of choices without any sense of how to
discriminate among those choices—how to transform their
choices into *informed* choices—are not fully free. They are in
the position of a tourist visiting France who cannot read French

but must select items from a French menu. That person must rely on someone else, a friend or a stranger, or choose blindly. In only a restricted sense is such a person "free"; that is, he is free only insofar as no one forces him to select a particular item from the menu. At least a minimal understanding of French is necessary in order to select an item that will suit the tourist's taste. At the very least, he must have knowledge in order to make informed choices. Until then, someone who can be presumed to know must help him choose.

Clearly, paternalism looms large at this point, and many are justifiably alarmed by this prospect. But a person who is ignorant requires the guidance of someone else who knows, or is in a better position to know, if he is to avoid the risk of making a serious mistake. We acknowledge this every time we visit a physician to combat an illness or take our car to the mechanic for repairs. If the mistake is nothing more than selecting the wrong item from a menu, the consequences will be slight—indigestion, perhaps, or disturbing dreams. But if the mistake involves serious choices, such as whether to take physics or Ping-Pong, the consequences may be more serious.

To be sure, the issue here is much larger than choices on a menu or occasional blunders in course selection. The issue has to do with empowerment, and the difficulty is to determine who, precisely, is to make the decisions that will realize that end, and what the grounds for those determinations are to be—especially if the person making the decision is not the person directly involved. In the context of education, to these issues we might add a third: what is the student's role in making the choices required or urged upon him? Let us take each of these difficulties in turn.

The question of who is to decide with or for the student (in the case of college courses) will be answered variously depending on the student's level of sophistication. The younger and less sophisticated the student—the greater his ignorance of French in reading the menu, if you will—the greater the assistance he requires in determining the right thing to do.

Now this is a loaded phrase and hearkens back to Rousseau's notion that one needs to "force some men to be free" by seeing to it that they do the "right" thing. But surely, though we might object to the use of the term "force" in this context, there is something to this. Medieval thinkers had much less difficulty with this sort of claim than we do, because in their view the paradigm of freedom was God's will, which is perfectly free, spontaneous, and, stemming as it does from His omniscience, results always in "the right thing." Thus, if one acts from ignorance, he will act unfreely and (in all likelihood) sin. Accordingly, it makes sense to "force" that person to do the right thing, which is, in the end, what the person himself truly wants to do. Still, the notion of force raises red flags in the consciousness of every modern (and postmodern) thinker, and well it should. But that is no reason to reject the notion out of hand. The heart of the matter is that one person may know better than another in a particular case what is best for that person. In such a case, it seems reasonable for the one who knows to try to persuade the one who might choose wrongly to do the right thing. Since the goal here is autonomy, force is out of the question, but good advice and persuasive argument are surely in order.

Even the great champion of negative liberty, John Stuart Mill, saw the need, on occasion, for one person to decide for another what might be best when the latter is "incapable of being acted on by rational consideration of distant motives."[3] Now our students may not be "incapable," but they are unsure and unaware of "distant motives." This is why the mentoring relationship, even at the university level, must involve an element of paternalism. Students do not know what they need in order to become educated persons, and while members of the faculty are certainly not infallible, they are in a better position to recommend and guide. In Rousseau's polity, this is the role of the legislator, and the goal in the two cases is the same: to enable people to become free agents.

A student's freedom, viewed positively, presupposes knowledge; it involves doing the "right thing," which is whatever the student truly needs—that is, whatever will help that person achieve positive freedom. To see this, we must recall the distinction made in the last chapter between the student's needs and his desires, since the two are not always the same. This distinction is critical to our present discussion.

If we were totally honest, we would admit that students may be clear about what they *want*, but for the most part they have no idea at all of what it is they *need* in order to become educated persons. As they confront their course schedules, they know they "need" to complete their major requirements, they "need" a course that fits into their schedule, they "need" an easy elective that won't reduce their GPA. But how many of these "needs" are genuine, and how many are bogus? No general answer is possible, of course, and this is where the mentor-advisor comes in, to help students realize those choices that will, in fact, accord with their real (human) needs. In the present context, those needs have to do with general requirements that realize the goals of a liberal education.

Unfortunately, the advisor may know as little as the student when it comes to general requirements. Typically, advisors will simply refer to the catalog or advisors' handbook to see what is required of all students without giving it any serious thought. But we must presume, in principle if not in fact, that the faculty member is in a better position to know what the student needs than is the student himself. (And this presumption would be warranted, in fact, if our academies paid greater attention to the important role of the advisor and required all faculty to address the questions basic to every student's education on a regular basis. I shall return to this point in the last chapter.)

Thus, for better or worse, it is the faculty members' responsibility in the typical four-year college to decide for the majority of students what their needs are as far as basic, general education is concerned. At lower levels, say in high school (contrary to current trends, which run in the opposite direction), this rule applies with even greater strictness. As students complete high school and pass through their undergraduate years, their own role should become greater as the faculty member's role changes from one who requires to one who recommends. This role changes as the student's sophistication and maturity increases, a sign that his freedom is increasing, as is his correlative responsibility for making his own choices. Ironically, the present system reverses this order, giving students maximum (negative) freedom during the first years only to take it away in the face of major requirements later on.

This argument will not be popular, since many will contend that it "sells the students short," and deprives them of the "freedom" to make those choices that affect their lives. But once again, this is a confusion of negative and positive freedom: it seems elementary to insist that students cannot make truly *free* choices if they are ignorant of what it is they choose, that is, if they are educational tourists picking blindly from the curricular menu. They cannot possibly know what will be valuable to them, in fact, until after they have made the choice, and then it may be too late. In such cases, they will feel cheated, as alumni sometimes let their alma maters know. Thus, even though the faculty are far from omniscient, they must take it upon themselves to help students do the right thing, to make those choices that will eventually set them free—from the faculty, in the short run, and from any uninvited outside influence, in the long run.

What, though, should be the grounds upon which general education decisions are made? As I shall argue, general education ought to focus on a core reading requirement. This brings us to the knotty question of the "canon," a concept that has come under serious criticism of late.

The term "canon" refers to a list of classic works or "Great Books" that are regarded as minimally required reading for all educated persons. For a variety of reasons, this claim is now seen by many as a presumption and the current movement is toward more "open" requirements, no requirements at all, or, at best, requirements that provide greater cultural variety (in the critics' view) than the traditional canon. In a word, the movement is toward a "multicultural" approach—if requirements are not to be eliminated altogether.

What is at issue, ultimately, is the question of how the canon is determined, that is, whether one can legitimately make the claim that *any* books are "great," and whether it is possible to judge a book to be a classic without introducing one's personal prejudice, thereby fostering "hegemony." Critics of the canon maintain that its constitutive books are written by dead white European males and are therefore fundamentally ideological, in that they foster a political perspective that is narrow and, for a great many students, irrelevant. That is, the canon is said to reflect what Robert Scholes has called "the rotting carcass of Western Civilization." Any attempt to describe a book (any book) as "great" is spurious, since it merely reflects one's personal, culturally determined perspective. Therefore, it is better if students are asked to read books that reflect a variety of cultural perspectives, especially perspectives that have too long been ignored.

Now there are two important and related questions here. To begin with, we must ask if (in fact) the canon is ideological. Secondly, we must ask why ideology in any form is anathema to education as it is defined here. The second question is the easier of the two, so I shall address it first. Since it is clear that a student can only become free if he is put into possession of his *own* mind, any sort of ideological approach to education flies in the face of that goal, leading as it does to indoctrination, not to freedom. Let me sharpen this distinction.

Thinking occurs only where there is ideational conflict or contradiction, when we are confronted by an idea that does not fit into our belief system. A class in which there is heated discussion characterized by disagreement and difference of opinion is one that is likely to engender thought. Though it may do so less effectively, as has been shown in recent psychological testing, a lecture may also encourage thought if the ideas strike the listener as new or different and disagreement with the speaker is not only allowed but encouraged. In contrast, a "we agree" session in which one or two basic themes are set forth dogmatically and discussion is led in one direction does not engender thought; such sessions instill a rigid set of beliefs that are not questioned, but simply remembered. The first scenario initiates the educational process, in that it frees the mind from the prison of fixed beliefs. The second is indoctrination in that it merely reinforces what we already believe to be true, or gives us a set of beliefs that we must somehow fit into a prearranged scheme we find comfortable (and comforting). For some, this may not be a problem, since their belief system already consists of conflicting sets of beliefs, internally inconsistent or even contradictory. For others, fitting new beliefs into an existing system may involve the removal of beliefs that they find comfortable, which can be unsettling. This is what is meant by the vague term "thinking": analysis, synthesis, problem-solving skills, to be sure, but also the ability to organize sets of beliefs into a coherent system that increases understanding. It is one of the main goals of education to help young minds systematize their thoughts coherently in conformity with independent standards.

In this regard, we can see how important it is to posit an objective truth independent of us, directing our thought, together with standards of reasonableness impressing our manner of thinking. Without truth and reasonableness we have nothing but conflicting belief systems, and each of us is vulnerable to coercion by another with stronger convictions, or a persuasive manner, whose only goal is conformity of opinion—those "thugs" who, as Mark Van Doren reminds us, "care only about what we think, not how we think."[4] If we agree that there is truth independent of any set of beliefs, our own or others', then dialogue makes inquiry purposive, directed toward beliefs that conform to things as they are rather than merely to another belief system. Genuine thought can arise only in a context in which open minds seek to know; it cannot happen when one presumes to know and makes it his or her goal to convince others.

The two scenarios we imagined a moment ago are as different from one another as can be. The first engenders thought, the second mere conformity of belief. Readings that are selected and taught because they present a variety of perspectives foster education; readings that are ideological, especially readings that fit into the teacher's own belief system, lead to indoctrination. An example of the latter is suggested in the description of a course offered at the University of Michigan in the fall of 1999. The course, "Issues in Afro-American Development: Affirmative Action," promises to "begin the process of cogent action and to develop the language to articulate affirmative action as a right and not a benefit." Clearly, whether or not we agree with it, a course with such a clearly stated ideological purpose is not designed to engender thought, but to direct behavior.

Thus, if the charge that the canon is ideological is well-founded, it is serious indeed. I shall ignore for the moment the question of non-canonical books that are clearly (and at times avowedly) ideological, since even the critics of the canon should agree, though many do not, that ideology in any form is unacceptable. The question I must face, however, is whether the canon of Western "high" culture is ideological because it presents a narrow, restricted cultural perspective. This charge, it seems to me, is false for several reasons.

To begin with, the charge attacks a straw man. There is no monolithic "canon" that presents a particular cultural perspective. We must first determine which list of books constituting the Canon of Western High Culture we are talking about, since there are many such lists. Should we rely on Mortimer Adler or Harold Bloom? Or perhaps the lists drawn up by faculty at places like Columbia, Notre Dame, or St. John's College? Whichever we choose, our initial impression is one of diversity of opinion and bewildering variety of perspective. But even if we narrow our attention to one list taken at random, we notice immediately that it comprises a heterogeneous group of books that speaks to us from diverse cultural perspectives, including, in many cases, non-Western perspectives. Most of the books considered great by the vast majority of those who have actually read them provide an astonishing variety of points of view on nearly every question ever pondered by perplexed men and women.

Seldom, if ever, can one find in "canonical" works of non-fiction, for example, any two authors who agree about much of anything. And when it comes to works of fiction, exceptional authors do not argue or seek to persuade to *any* particular point of view. The heart and soul of good fiction is its essential ambiguity, due in no small measure to the level of generality that great fiction achieves. For example, even though a novel or a play depicts particular persons, what they have to say is true of such persons generally. Hamlet, in this regard, is an individual in a play. But he is also a token of a type—the melancholy youth, the sensitive youth, the troubled youth, etc. He is all of

these at once, which is what makes the play at its center am-
biguous and open to a variety of interpretations. Great writers
speak with many voices, not one.

Richard Posner, to draw attention to the fact that authors
of such works do not preach or take sides, has called this characteristic of great works of literature "impartiality." Posner writes:

> Forgoing the facile triumph, the author [of great literary works]
> makes the reader see the situation from the villain's point of
> view too. To visualize a Jew [in *The Merchant of Venice*] as fully if
> wickedly human was something few Elizabethans could have
> done; Shakespeare's great contemporary Marlowe could not
> do it. To portray Satan [in *Paradise Lost*] as a heroic figure, Milton
> was bordering on blasphemy. The *Iliad* is the oldest surviving
> expression of awareness that foreigners who are your mortal
> enemies might nevertheless have the same feelings as you.
> Hemingway "refuses to make villains of all the Fascists in *For
> Whom The Bell Tolls* or to make all the Loyalists good and de-
> cent people." Stendahl, as hostile as he was to the Church and
> the nobility, refuses in *The Red and The Black* to romanticize
> liberals, peasants, republicans, bourgeois, Parisians or provincials,
> or Bonapartists.[5]

Great literature cannot be reduced to a single message without leaving a significant residue, because in every case it "in-
vites a variety of *incompatible* moral responses."[6] Which is the
"correct" response? The answer is arbitrary, at best. And the
reason for this is that great literature is art; that is, in fiction

ideas have taken on dramatic form, thus engaging imagination along with thought. Whatever ideas we find in great fiction, drama, or poetry have been "set with a complex interlocutatory process such that [insights] are never the 'final vocabulary' of individual works."[7]

This is not to imply that authors of great works of drama or fiction do not have a point of view or that great novels or plays do not at times express outrage. Fiction cannot be judged solely on formal grounds, though I would argue that those grounds are central to the work *as a work of art.* In saying this, I seek to distance myself somewhat from Oscar Wilde, who insisted that "there is no such thing as a moral or an immoral book. Books are well written or badly written. That is all."[8] I think this is an overstatement: great works of fiction can be "moralistic," and take a stand on important issues. But that stand is not the measure of the book, and it must be presented in such a way that it provokes thought and not mere reaction in the reader. The fiction of Charles Dickens is an interesting case in point.

Dickens manages, for the most part, to moralize without preaching. His novels are certainly didactic, however, and the author has a difficult time remaining impartial and controlling his strong feelings. In *Hard Times*, for example, he is opposed to labor unions; his anti-Semitism shows through in *Oliver Twist* and *Little Dorrit*, and virtually all of his novels are sexist, in that his female characters tend to be, for the most part, silly, empty-headed, and lacking a strong voice. There are further difficulties with Dickens's novels as well. He is frequently downright sentimental, and his characters tend to be two-dimensional, very good or very bad, with little room in the middle. The reason for this, one suspects, is Dickens's sharp eye for satire, which is always on the alert; satire, directed as it is to specific targets, does not blend well with art. Furthermore, Dickens's characters tend to remain unchanged throughout his novels, and even that notable exception, Scrooge, changes so dramatically and quickly that it stretches the reader's credulity to the limits. For these reasons I would hesitate to agree that Dickens is a writer of the very first rank.

On the other hand, he has written a number of books that must be considered exceptional, because they do provoke thought about serious subjects, because his moralizing tends to be unobtrusive and always couched in a powerful prose style, because he has a lively imagination that can produce extraordinary twists and turns in his plots, and because he is an exceptional writer and storyteller. His characters, if not always believable, are always memorable. Furthermore, some of his descriptions are riveting, and his wit and humor blend in captivating ways with his social commentary to bring considerable balance and harmony to his novels.

Examples of his descriptive powers can be found throughout his novels, even in the earliest ones, written when he was still struggling with the serialized format and the youthful sentiment that sometimes flawed his prose. In *The Old Curiosity Shop,* for example (which is certainly not one of his better novels), we find the following description of the London that Nell and her grandfather have just left behind them. Note how it reflects Dickens's hatred of urban London and his love of the pastoral, and note also how he raises these feelings to the level of art:

> At length these streets, becoming more straggled yet, dwindled and dwindled away, until there were only small garden patches bordering the road, with many a summer house innocent of paint and built of old timber or some fragment of a boat, green as the tough cabbage stalks that grew about it, and grottoes at the seams with toad-stools and tight-sticking snails. To these succeeded pert cottages, two and two with plots of ground in front, laid out in angular beds with stiff box borders and narrow paths between, where footsteps never strayed to make the gravel rough.... Then came a turnpike; then fields again with trees and haystacks; then a hill; and on top of that the traveler might stop, and—looking back at old St. Pauls looming through the smoke, its cross peeping above the cloud (if the day were clear) and glittering in the sun; and casting his eyes upon the Babel out of which it grew until he traced it down to the furthest outposts of the invading army of bricks and mortar whose station lay for the present nearly at his feet— might feel at last that he were clear of London.[9]

As we can plainly see, Dickens succeeds on aesthetic grounds, whether or not we can detect the author hiding in the thicket of words.

There is a line that great authors hesitate to cross between moral commitment, on the one hand, and outrage that collapses into didacticism and "preachiness," on the other. Great literature contributes to a liberal education precisely because it forces the reader to think for herself and does not drag her, at times unknowingly, toward a foregone conclusion. Harold Bloom's comment about George Eliot's moralistic stand in *Middlemarch* is much to the present point. Bloom notes that Eliot's aesthetic secret is "her mastery of what James, reviewing her in 1866, called 'a certain middle field where morals and aesthetics move in concert.' Perhaps it is not so much a secret as it is George Eliot herself, since I can think of no other major novelist, before or since, whose moralizings constitute an aesthetic virtue rather than a disaster."[10]

While Dickens must be considered one exception to Bloom's generalization, there is surely one more, namely, Jane Austen, who also flirts with didacticism in her novels. In *Mansfield Park*, for example, Fannie Price has strong reservations about the romantic advances of Henry Crawford—and faults Crawford's sister as well—because he is short on character: his actions show a lack of "principles." The Aristotelian influence in this novel is particularly strong as, despite the affability and affection both Crawfords show toward Fanny, their lack of what Aristotle would have called "moral virtue" makes it impossible for her to reciprocate their feelings. In the end, she turns out to be correct, as Henry runs off with Fanny's married cousin and Mary Crawford destroys Edmund's deep affection for her by trying to convince him to help her "cover up" the embarrassing event. As always, for Austen, restraint and self-control mark the exceptional person, rather than "good breeding" or fine manners. This thoroughly Aristotelian theme is apparent throughout the novel. At the same time, Austen's aesthetic impartiality requires that she depict the character of Henry Crawford in a sympathetic way: he is not altogether a terrible person and he does, after all, have the good sense to fall in love with Fanny.

The same sense of balance and response to the requirements of impartiality are evidenced in Austen's earlier novel, *Sense and Sensibility,* in which the character of John Willoughby is depicted as sympathetic and caring, for all his lack of self-control (again). The same can be said for the object of his affection, Marianne Dashwood, who is flighty and passionate—to the point of mania—but who is also loving and capable of growth, as shown by her dawning realization of what a good soul the silly Mrs. Jennings is and how much she is devoted to both Marianne and Elinor Dashwood. None of these characters, except Elinor, reaches the high standards Jane

Austen holds up to her characters, but they are all nevertheless carefully drawn and worthy of the reader's affection. One suspects that Austen herself had many of the same feelings toward these characters that Elinor had toward John Willoughby when the latter revealed his genuine affection for Marianne near the end of the novel. At the time, Elinor was torn between compassion for his suffering and outrage regarding his way of treating her sister.

Jane Austen's feel for irony is not as strong in either of these novels as it is in the superior *Pride and Prejudice*, but her consummate writing skills, her eye for psychological nuance, and her sense of the comic mark even these novels as exceptional. Once again, it is the sense of balance emphasized by Harold Bloom that separates Austen from the rest of the pack. Like Dickens (though more so, in my view), Austen is simply a master of her craft. Such mastery offsets the occasional slip into didacticism that would ruin a lesser novelist.

Great writers manage to maintain that balance, somehow, or at least to do homage to the aesthetic despite the moral concern they feel deeply. Indeed, it is precisely the demands of the aesthetic that allow the novelist to remain in control of the material. As Flaubert once said, it is discipline that makes art of impulse.

This is important to note, because, as mentioned, novels are above all works of art, and aesthetic criteria are paramount.

Some would regard this as mere formalism, but formal considerations are germane to fiction, and it is a mistake to reject them altogether out of a blind regard for what the author has to say. I shall return to this point in a moment.

When we turn to those works of nonfiction that are considered great or "canonical," any two taken at random diverge at nearly every point. Take Plato and Aristotle: despite their proximity in time and place, they are poles apart on almost every basic philosophical issue. Even on the question of the place of women in society, one finds Plato taking the remarkably modern view that women should not be denied the right to rule in the ideal society. Aristotle, on the other hand, falls back on the orthodox sexist view of women as inferior to men. One could go on to point out innumerable instances of disagreement between the two men, and between them and almost every other philosopher who followed them.

There are many benefits to be taken away from a reading of great thinkers, one of which is most assuredly the realization that the search for truth is a meandering, twisted, and uncertain one and no one knows precisely where it leads. This is a decidedly non-ideological consequence, and these works can hardly be said to place intellectual blinders on their readers. On the contrary. One must wonder when one hears such criticisms of the canon whether the critic has actually read the books. I am reminded in this regard of Martin Luther's hatred of "the classics" because they did not suit his taste: he felt awkward in their presence. The only way these sorts of criticisms make any sense at all is if one stands back at a great distance; once one ventures into range of the books themselves, one is impressed above all else by the variety of points of view that must be said to provoke thought, not to mold it.

The most serious criticism of the canon, however, is the one that insists that any list of required books must represent marginalized thinkers—minorities and women, chiefly. My initial response to this objection is to ask, again, which list we are referring to, since if we refer to Harold Bloom's list, the question is moot. His list includes numerous women and otherwise "marginalized" thinkers, from Jane Austen and Simone de Beauvoir, on the one hand, to Najib Mahfuz and R. K. Narayan, on the other.

But two more serious questions lie behind this criticism. On the one hand, can one decide which books to add to the list(s) without reflecting *some* sort of ideology? If it cannot be done, any educational program that involves such lists will invariably be little more than a disguised form of indoctrination. Critics of the canon who voice this objection apparently think that since ideology is inevitable their brand is preferable, and they are quick to draw up their own lists of required reading. But, again, the deeper question is whether such lists are *invari-

ably ideological. I think they are not, if the books are selected for the right reasons. This brings us to the second problem, one that is more challenging: on what grounds does one decide what books are to be included on such a list?

The answer to this question is as obvious as it is unacceptable to critics of the canon. Decisions must be made on the basis of whether or not the books deserve to be included. Works of nonfiction must be seminal and historically significant— even if somehow "wrong," like Adam Smith's *Wealth of Nations* or Karl Marx's *Capital*. Works of fiction, on the other hand, must be exemplary: well written, thought-provoking, and symptomatic of the heights the human imagination can reach. All books, fiction or nonfiction, must be original as well. Harold Bloom suggests that great books must be "strange" in their originality. This seems an attractive notion, since such books would stand out in any crowd.

I do not wish to imply that all of the arguments of the critics of the canon are silly or fallacious. This is not so. One cannot deny, for instance, that the weight of opinion about literature can be shifted by "opinion-makers," including critics and editors of magazines and journals, or that determinations of "greatness" are subject to the vicissitudes of time and place. Books that are regarded as canonical are so, in part at least, because opinion about them has become rigid over time and, in some cases, is no longer questioned. If all they had done was to question this inertial tendency among list-makers, post-modern critics would have to be thanked for waking tradionalists out of their doldrums. But this is not all they have done, and their resentment has gotten the better of them.

The question that must be faced is why certain books stand up to the test of time. The answer is not that "establishment axiologists," in Barbara Herrnstein Smith's phrase, have mandated it, but that certain works really are better than others.

Richard Posner has tried to walk in this intellectual minefield in his *Law and Literature*, and while he leans toward the view of many postmodern critics that the test of time is basically "Darwinian," he insists that certain books exhibit "universality." It is universality, or "permanent features of the human condition," that in the end constitutes greatness, in Posner's view.[11] Certain works of narrative fiction exhibit these features, others do not. I think Posner is correct, but I would add the other formal criteria mentioned above, including Bloom's notion of "strange originality." To be sure, originality is a mark of true genius, but it is one that can only be detected by those who have read a great deal. To one who has read little, everything seems original.

These considerations do not, of course, "prove" that some works are better than others, but they provide rational grounds for the winnowing of reasons supporting the claim of genuine worth. I would simply note that the lack of proof (in the narrow sense) does not imply the absence of rational standards. A claim can be reasonable without being certain. The conclusion that since greatness cannot be proved it cannot be argued is unwarranted, though popular of late.

If previously marginalized thinkers and writers are to be included on the lists of required reading, and clearly some should be, they must pass the acid test: they must be exceptional. To quote Bloom once again, "The Western Canon will never close, but it cannot be forced open by our current cheerleaders. Strength alone can open it up, the strength of a Freud or a Kafka, persistent in their cognitive negations."[12] We play a zero-sum game: if one book is placed on the list, another must be removed. In addition, students will read very few books in their four years as undergraduates, and may read even fewer after that, so these determinations are of considerable importance.

The reason the critics of the canon find this response unsatisfactory, however, is because they do not think it is possible to make disinterested aesthetic judgments and select books without one's biases showing through. Invariably, it will be argued, such lists reflect the prejudices of those who draw them up—usually white, European males who dominate the intellectual establishment. But this objection will not hold up to criticism, because, as I have argued, such lists do not foster *any* particular "point of view." Furthermore, it is possible to engage in aesthetic discussions and resolve them by appealing to reasonable standards that cannot be dismissed as nothing more than personal preferences.

The alternative notion, that a book should be included simply because it "represents" a missing point of view, is a weak claim and is untenable from the perspective on education I have articulated here. Such a position is purely political, not pedagogical, and it does not have the student's best interest in view. Books selected on political grounds will almost certainly lead to indoctrination—especially if they are selected by faculty who choose them because they agree with the author's point of view. From a pedagogical perspective, this is the worst possible reason for making such a selection, because it places the student in a bind. In such circumstances, students will almost certainly lack the courage to counter an older, more articulate teacher armed with a grade book and surrounded by like-minded students, who have strong attachments to the views of the author of a required text. But if the student does not feel free to disagree, he will never learn to think for himself, but will simply mouth his version of what the teacher told him to think. Faculty may enjoy this, but it is clearly a form of indoctrination. The grounds on which readings are selected are as important as the question of what is selected. Let me be more specific.

Consider the reasons we might give for choosing Goethe's *Faust* over Mary Shelley's *Frankenstein*. This is an interesting case because these two thinkers are both "Romantic" and seem to share a common fear of the threat of scientism. I say "seem" because Goethe's case is not as clear as Shelley's. And this, in a word, is why Goethe's book is a better choice to engender real thought in the minds of young readers.

Shelley finds it difficult to be the least bit sympathetic with Victor Frankenstein's love of science, describing it in terms that make it resemble a mania rather than a passion. To be sure, a passion for science (like any passion) can become a mania, and that is at least part of what Shelley wants to point out. The problem is that this point is too clear, not to say simplistic, and does not invite questioning when, in fact, the passion of the scientist for his work is truly different from the passion an artist, sculptor, or poet feels for his. Certainly, it is no less respectable.

In point of fact, Shelley's depiction of Victor Frankenstein is more a caricature than a character study, reflecting the book's overall tendency toward contrived circumstance, implausible exaggeration, and outrageous coincidence. In themselves, these are serious flaws in the book considered as a work of art, and would be considered such even in a book better written than this.

Contrast this with Goethe's visionary work, which can be seen as an attack on science and philosophy as well—the "despised logos" of Romantic and postmodern thinkers. Goethe's attack is more restrained and balanced than Shelley's, perhaps because of the poet's own ambivalence toward science. We must recall that Goethe knew science from the inside—he does not merely hold it at arm's length. He was himself an accomplished scientist who made a number of discoveries in optics, botany, and biology, where he anticipated aspects of modern evolutionary theory.

Be that as it may, if *Faust* is read as an attack against science, it cannot be considered altogether successful. Recall that after Faust leaves his study—turning his back forever on the life of the mind to follow his heart (and Mephistopheles)—he destroys several innocent people: Margaret in the first part of the poem, and, in Part Two, a stranger along with an elderly couple he has Mephisto "remove" from land he hopes to reclaim from the sea. He does not fare so well when he turns his back on science and philosophy. He never achieves the balance that Goethe seems to regard as central to human happiness.

Goethe's attack on scientistic man—his unrestrained thirst for knowledge, his lust for power over nature, his intellectual and emotional instability, and his failure in love (as noted by Erich Heller)—is not altogether successful, because it is never clear, in the poem itself, that Faust was wise to leave his study, despite his state of mind at the time. Much of the entertainment Mephisto arranges for him is silly and would leave a modern undergraduate yawning. Furthermore, in spite of himself, Faust is an interesting, complex, and even likable fellow.

We must never forget that, in the end, God intercedes and takes Faust into heaven. In the final analysis, Goethe's impartiality, his limitless imagination coupled with his control of the subject matter, and his unflinching honesty and heightened powers as a poet demand that he deliver a work that defies summary or reduction to a formula. Therefore, the reader is required to think about what Goethe says, having deeply engaged the poem on its own terms. *Faust* is a great work of art; *Frankenstein* is not, though it is (admittedly) a "good read."

Certainly, a gifted teacher could use Shelley's novel to engender discussion and get young people to think. But the subject matter is so one-sided that the reader must work through thick feelings of anger against Victor Frankenstein, if not all of science. This is a major shortcoming of works that express strong feelings. It is easier to wallow in such feelings than to work through them to achieve genuine thought. In this sense, *Faust* is nearly foolproof. It does not require a gifted teacher to provide a broader framework within which to discuss the material objectively and fairly. That is one of the reasons why such books should be included in the canon: they will survive even the worst of teachers, because the books are themselves the best of teachers.

The problem here is that Shelley feels so deeply about her subject (and admittedly she has more concerns than merely the attack on modern science) that she spells it out for the reader rather than demanding that the reader decide for himself where he stands on complex issues raised in the novel. It is difficult to defend the scientist to a young person who has only this novel to weigh against an almost total ignorance of the history of science, along with rather limited experience in struggling with serious scientific problems in the laboratory. Mary Shelley's novel suffers from the same one-sided view of science and human reason (one that saw science and reason as excluding imagination) that was typical of the Romantics generally. Postmodernism, in this regard, is simply the latest face of Romanticism and suffers from the same distorted view of human reason.

If we imagine Marilyn French, Catherine MacKinnon, or Peggy McIntosh, for example, teaching Shelley's novel—or, perhaps a novel by Maxine Hong Kingston, who is a better writer than Shelley—we must ask how much real thought will take place. We need not doubt how deeply the sense of outrage will run, however, and, in Kingston's case, how deep the teachers' sympathies will lie with the author. The same can be said of an African American teacher reading novels by James Baldwin or Chinua Achebe with his students, as we shall see in the next chapter. This is not to say that such readings are a "bad" thing and should be curtailed; it simply means that what happens has little to do with genuine education. These readings may evoke strong feelings in the students and engender lively (one-sided?) discussions. But this should not be confused with real thought, which can become nothing more than self-indulgence unless it is open-ended and sifted through the fine weave of emotional distance and respect for the antithesis.

Once again, what one must look for is balance and ambivalence on the author's part. Though strong feelings may not in themselves be a bad thing when properly directed, it is precisely the puzzlement and wonder that arise from conflicting ideas that lead, in the end, to real thought. These, in turn, cannot be found unless there is genuine dialogue, involving serious disagreement—within and among texts as well as in the classroom—coupled with an honest desire to find a truth that no one claims to hold firmly in hand at the outset. The alternative is books selected for their "message" taught by a true believer whose primary goal is to drive that message home.

In saying this, I hasten to add in closing this chapter that I do not advocate a merely formalist approach to the reading and teaching of literature—of the type that Martha Nussbaum so vehemently opposes. Nor do I think it possible to approach great literature with a political and ethical blank slate. None of us is completely neutral when it comes to dealing with serious questions taken up by serious novelists. However, Nussbaum (for one) is wrong when she suggests that one is *either* a mere formalist *or* has a "political agenda."[13] This is a false dichotomy. It is possible to approach literature in a manner that combines aesthetic and ethical-political concerns (witness Nussbaum herself when she actually engages in criticism). As Wayne Booth has pointed out, a critical attitude is perfectly compatible with immersion in the work, and complete involvement (immersion) in the work is not possible without engaging the content of the novel.

At the same time, my position would not allow us to select books for their "message" any more than it would allow us to use those books to convert students to the teacher's way of thinking. What is of concern here, as it is throughout, is to put students into possession of their *own* minds, not the minds of their teachers. Education leads to freedom; indoctrination leads to parroting.

The best way to avoid the latter is to select only great books. But even the best of these books can be reduced to "message" if the reader is determined. The temptation to do this is greatest if the reader happens to think that message is true—or false. This is what I meant earlier when I said that great books are "nearly" foolproof.

In the following chapter I shall show what happens when a reader approaches a great piece of literature with blinders on. If that reader happens to be a teacher, the result will be one that stands in direct opposition to the genuine end of liberal education, which presupposes open dialogue focusing on many-valued readings of the first order.

Chapter IV

HOW NOT TO READ A BOOK

"We are destroying all intellectual and aesthetic standards in the humanities and social sciences in the name of social justice."
—Harold Bloom

Chinua Achebe, whose vantage point puts him much closer to the issue than most critics, is outraged by the fact that Joseph Conrad is a "bloody racist" and concludes, as a result, that *Heart of Darkness* cannot be regarded as a great work of art. Achebe makes his claim quite clear:

> ...[T]he question is whether a novel which celebrates [the dehumanization of Africa and Africans], which depersonalizes a portion of the human race, can be called a great work of art. My answer is: No, it cannot.... I am talking about a book which parades in the most vulgar fashion prejudices and insults from which a section of mankind has suffered untold agonies and atrocities in the past and continues to do so in many ways and many places today. I am talking about a story in which the very humanity of black people is called into question. It seems to

me totally inconceivable that great art or even good art could possibly reside in such unwholesome surroundings.[1]

As is obvious, Chinua Achebe brings to the task of literary criticism a strong sense of outrage and conviction. In this regard, he joins other postmodern thinkers who dominate the current critical scene. I shall attempt to show that these feelings interfere with his ability to hear what the author has to say. The result is bad criticism and, if pursued in the classroom, bad teaching.

For better or worse, the academy is currently overrun by critics like Achebe, including such odd bedfellows as feminist, Marxist, psychoanalytic, deconstructionist, and reader-response critics. To this list we might add what I would call "Afrocentric critics," of which Achebe is perhaps the foremost example. What these critics have in common is that they stand outside the novel and look in on it from a jaundiced perspective that only permits them to see what they are looking for. That is to say, such postmodern critics, in reaction to the school of New Criticism that was pre-eminent in the 1950s and 1960s, bring their own ideological baggage with them when they read a novel, insisting as they do that interpretation is always covertly political anyway. But this is a half-truth. It is possible to reduce (if not eliminate) elements of ideology in criticism, though one must first allow that it can be done. Not all critics have axes to grind. In any event, since, in the words of Richard Rorty, many postmodern critics "are in it for what they can get out of it, not for the satisfaction of getting something right,"[2] it is not surprising that such critics can only see what they want to see.

One such critic is Robin West, who is convinced that the heroes of Franz Kafka's fictional world are victims of capitalist exploitation. This gives her criticism an interesting and original slant, but it is not clear that she has anything important to say about the fiction of Franz Kafka. Richard Posner has taken West to task for what he regards as her misreading of Kafka.[3] Judge Posner, who seems to have read everything ever written, is a formalist in spite of himself and, like the New Critics, insists that we approach the novel on its own terms. He has shown quite clearly the dangers that arise when a reader such as West approaches Kafka with her mind made up about what she will find.

This is not to say that novels do not allow for multiple interpretations—they do, as I noted in the last chapter. But there are some interpretations that can be ruled out because they are far-fetched: they seem to have no ties with what the author has said in the text. Posner shows that this is indeed the case with West's readings of Kafka.

What Judge Posner has done with Robin West's reading of Kafka I shall attempt to do here with Chinua Achebe's reading of Joseph Conrad's novella *Heart of Darkness*. I hope to show how Achebe has read racism into Conrad's extraordinary novella, and, in the process, show why this approach is anathema to literature considered as a work of art. In the process, it will become clear why teachers who approach literature the way Achebe does are liable to force their own way of seeing upon their students and thereby mitigate the student's own lively imagination and independence of thought—both of which are essential for the appreciation of great literature and the realization of the goals of a liberal education.

Achebe has shown in his novel *Things Fall Apart* that we tread on dangerous ground when we label whole societies as "primitive" or "uncivilized." The argument in his critique of *Heart of Darkness* seeks, among other things, to further that line of thought. This he has done quite convincingly. What Achebe has not done in his critique, however, is to argue convincingly that Conrad's attitude toward the "primitive" people he describes in his novel makes it impossible for us to consider the novel "great." The reason for this, in my view, is that Achebe fails to see in Conrad's novel the conflicts and ambiguities that make it an exceptional work of art. Achebe sees elements of racism, which are indeed there, but he seems oblivious to the ambivalence toward both race and Western civilization nesting within the narrator's contempt for the exploitation and greed that he sees as endemic to Europe. In this regard, two things need to be made clear: (1) the novel's racism is not as prevalent as Achebe maintains, and it is certainly not strong enough to flaw the novel as a work of art; and (2) "greatness" in art can be present in spite of elements of racism as long as there are other mitigating factors that make alternative interpretations possible and reasonable. Let us consider each of these points in turn.

I shall begin by listing the full range of objections Achebe raises to show that Conrad is a racist and *therefore* cannot have written a great novel. We must separate at the outset the author, Conrad, from the narrator (and hero) of the tale, Marlow. Achebe does not do this, and this confusion weakens the seven main objections he raises to Conrad's novella. (1) Conrad's [Marlow's] frequent use of the term "nigger." (2) Conrad's [that is, the author's] "problem with niggers," as deduced from his own account of his first encounter with a black man (320). (3) Conrad's [Marlow's] descriptions of Africans as "just limbs or rolling eyes" and his unwillingness to let them speak. (4) Conrad's [Marlow's] treatment of the "Amazon woman," whom Achebe sees as "a savage counterpart" to "the refined, European woman" with whom the story will end (317). (5) Conrad's [Marlow's] description of the fireman. (6) Kurtz's apparent mastery over the natives, "thus reducing Africa to the role of props for the breakup of one petty European mind" (319). (7) The novel's overall "dehumanization [of Africans] which depersonalizes a portion of the human race" (319).

Achebe is certainly correct in saying that Conrad uses the term "nigger" with reckless abandon. At least, he is correct in saying that Marlow does so; Achebe never really differentiates between the author and his protagonist. The question is whether Marlow's language signifies anything of importance to Achebe's overall argument. I think not, because nothing whatever follows about either Conrad or Conrad's novel from the fact that his protagonist uses an offensive term in referring to the natives of the Congo.

To begin with, Marlow's usage of the term "nigger" may not imply that Marlow himself considers the term demeaning or insulting. One suspects he uses the term as he might any other, since the word certainly didn't carry the same emotional charge in the late-nineteenth century as it does today. Even if we could make the label "racist" stick to Marlow, however, it would not allow us to infer anything whatever about Conrad or attribute the term "racist" to Conrad's novel. It would take Atlas working with Hercules to move the argument from the premise that Marlow is a racist to the conclusion that either Conrad or Conrad's novel is racist: the gulf is too wide. It is quite possible, for example, that Conrad is holding Marlow's racism up to ridicule—just as he seems to be undermining the European preference for the color white in a number of interesting ways in the novel.[4] In any event, Marlow's racism is not necessarily Conrad's. Nor need it flaw the novel as a whole.

We need to turn to Achebe's other arguments.

It might be said in connection with several of Achebe's points that Conrad was simply describing what he saw and incorporating his own experience into the novel, which we know contains biographical elements. In this regard, his descriptions of the native people he saw are not intentionally denigrating: they are intended to be descriptions of people and events he encountered and experienced. Despite the fact that the lens he looks through had been ground in Europe by white craftsmen, in the novel the poet merely described what he saw. The racist elements in this case would be, at best, inadvertent, which is to say present, but hardly a "celebration" of the dehumanization of Africa.

To this argument Achebe responds that he "will not trust the evidence even of a man's very eyes when I suspect them to be as jaundiced as Conrad's" (322). Presumably, it is the author's "problem with niggers," as mentioned above, that Achebe has in mind here. Unfortunately, the argument is a *non sequitur,* because whatever Conrad's personal problems might be, his protagonist is not necessarily seeing the world through Conrad's eyes. The issue is whether Marlow is a racist, and even if this is the case (and it may be so) it might pay to listen to what he has to say; even the most jaundiced eye occasionally sees things the rest of us have overlooked.

But, more to our present point, it will not do to argue, as Achebe does, that Conrad ignores features of Africa that would conflict with the image he is determined to present. This is doubtlessly the case, but what is central to the novel is not what Conrad does not see, but what he does see, and subsequently incorporates into his novel. We must bear in mind that Conrad is describing a part of Marlow's experience of the Congo. But it is just that; it is *part* of that experience, and it is Marlow's experience. I shall return to this point below.

Achebe objects to Conrad's "bestowal of human expression to [Kurtz's Intended] and the withholding of it from [Kurtz's African mistress]" (317). In fact, Achebe objects to the fact that the natives who surround Marlow are silent or speak only briefly in pidgin English. But this might be easily explained by the fact that conversation with "the Amazon" (to use Achebe's term) is impossible under the circumstances and, generally, Marlow does not speak the native language and cannot possibly engage in conversation with these people. In addition, expression may not be such a great thing in this novel: much of what the white people who surround Marlow have to say reveals them to be narrow, stupid, greedy, ambitious, and bigoted—and this goes for Marlow himself at times. In any event, language does not exhaust the whole of "expression," and what the "Amazon" does *not* say is wonderfully eloquent. The vision of the "barbarous and superb woman [who] did not so much as flinch, and stretched tragically her bare arms after us over the somber and glittering river" is much more engaging than Conrad's sketchy description of Kurtz's frail and self-deluded fiancee at the end of the novel.[5] Whether this description of Kurtz's "Intended" is strictly correct, it is certainly possible for this woman to be viewed in this light—and critics have done so—and the contrast between this woman and Kurtz's "Amazon" can easily be reversed in favor of the black woman, who is magnificent. In fact, this possible reversal is essential to the novel, as we shall see. But there are other areas of uncertainty in the novel that result, one suspects, from Conrad's quite genuine revulsion over what he found when he actually visited the Congo himself and experienced firsthand "the vilest scramble for loot that ever disfigured the history of human conscience and geographical exploration."[6]

Achebe unfairly dismisses Conrad's revulsion, as expressed through his narrator, as "bleeding heart sentiments," but there are good grounds for believing that they are the real thing. Not only do we have Conrad's comments quoted above but there are numerous passages in the book that bear out Marlow's initial claim that

The conquest of the earth, which means mostly the taking it away from those who have a different complexion or slightly flatter noses than ourselves, is not a pretty thing when you look at it too much.[7]

Consider, further, the unfavorable aspect things European convey. Marlow arrives in the Congo to find upturned and rusting machinery in the midst of a verdant wilderness into which black people crawl to lick their wounds and to escape their white "masters" who beat them for no reason. Marlow himself is no great shakes, self-absorbed and a bit smug; and neither are the faceless "pilgrims" who cluster, mutter, and scheme among themselves. These same people later fire their rifles stupidly into the brush to scare off the natives who attack the boat, and later boast of their courage in the face of danger. But more ridiculous still are the chief accountant with his "collars, his vast cuffs, his brushed hair," with his books in apple-pie order, appearing for all the world "like a hairdresser's dummy"; the brick-maker who hadn't made any bricks for a year; the agent whom Marlow describes as a "papier-maché Mephistopheles"; and Kurtz's disciple, the "harlequin" who is every bit the fool, dashing off into the bush with a book on seamanship in one pocket of his patchwork coat and cartridges in the other, despite the fact that he has neither boat nor weapon! The characters who people this book are not admirable folk—except for the cannibals, to whom I shall return in a moment.

We must first consider Achebe's point that Africa is being exploited to form a "prop for the breakup of one petty European mind." Surely, this is an oversimplification. What Conrad is doing is to use a portion of Africa, to wit, that portion that is relatively undeveloped and in the process of being raped by greedy Europeans, to provide a backdrop against which we can witness Marlow's journey into the heart of darkness. In that journey we discover Marlow's essential likeness to the corrupted Kurtz, who represents the "best" that Europe can produce and who has become more savage than the most savage of the black people he manages, somehow, to control. But Kurtz's ability to lord over these people is no comment on their gullibility or simplicity. Kurtz has a hold over everyone, apparently, even some he has not met, such as Marlow. What happens to Kurtz in Africa is less a comment on the Africans than it is on the faintness of the line that separates the primitive people from the highly civilized and much-touted European Kurtz, whose "mother [let us recall] was half-English, his father was half-French. All Europe contributed to the making of Kurtz."[8] It is simply not clear, from the novel, just who is "superior" to whom.

This same ambivalence, not only toward civilization but also toward race, shows itself in Marlow's discussions about the fireman. Achebe quotes Marlow at length, and I shall follow suit:

> ...[B]etween whiles I had to look at the savage who was the fireman. He was an improved specimen; he could fire up a vertical boiler. He was there below me, and, upon my word, to look at him was as edifying as seeing a dog in a parody of breeches and a feather hat, walking on his hind legs. A few

months of training had done for that really fine chap. He squinted at the steam gauge and at the water gauge with an evident effort of intrepidity—and he had filed his teeth, too, the poor devil, and the wool of his pate shaved into queer patterns, and three ornamental scars on each of his cheeks. He ought to have been clapping his hands and stamping his feet on the bank, instead of which he was hard at work, a thrall to strange witchcraft, full of improving knowledge.[9]

Clearly, there are racist slurs in this description of the fireman who looks "like a dog in a parody of breeches and a feather hat, walking on hind legs...." But note that this sentence is immediately followed by, "A few months of training had done for that really fine chap," a comment that reflects admiration for a man who learned quickly.

Later, we find another interesting attitudinal conflict when Marlow notes that "he ought to have been clapping his hands and stamping his feet on the bank, instead of which he was hard at work, a thrall to strange witchcraft, full of improving knowledge." The fireman is like a walking dog, yet he is a "really fine chap." Then, this "savage" who was enthralled by the engine is "hard at work" and "full of improving knowledge." We know Conrad identified work and knowledge, along with "restraint," as the positive elements of civilization, and yet we find them exhibited in the behavior of the fireman. The ideas juxtaposed in this manner suggest a struggle within the novelist's own mind. These struggles are worked over by the

poetic imagination and surface in mixed messages and conflicting images.

These tensions and conflicts are central to the novel and
can be found throughout: racist elements cluster beside elements of admiration, approval, and possibly even affection. But
Achebe does not see these latter elements. He is fixed on the
racist elements and he therefore misses the conflicts that are
fundamental to the novel. This can be shown even more clearly
in light of Achebe's comments about the death of the helmsman. Achebe quotes Marlow, in part, as follows:

> And the intimate profundity of that look he gave me when
> he received his hurt remains to this day in my memory—like
> a claim of distant kinship affirmed in a supreme moment
> (Achebe, 316).

Achebe admits that Marlow feels a "distant kinship" for
the black man, but he puts backspin on this admission by saying that Marlow resents the fact that the black man "lays a claim
on the white man which is well-nigh intolerable." This is simply not clear from the passage, especially in light of the fact that
Marlow considers that moment "supreme." There are many
reasons why a memory cannot be erased, but they do not,
normally, include the fact that they are "intolerable." On the
contrary, intolerable memories are erased as quickly as possible, or buried deep within the subconscious mind.

It is interesting in this regard that in selecting this portion of Marlow's comment, Achebe ignores several sentences that precede it. The context of these remarks is revealing. In the novel, Marlow begins by telling his listeners

> I missed my late helmsman awfully—I missed him while his body was still lying in the pilot house....Well, don't you see, he had done something, he had steered; for months I had him at my back—a help—an instrument. It was a kind of partnership. He steered for me—I had to look after him, I was worried about his deficiencies, and thus a subtle bond had been created, of which I only became aware when it was suddenly broken.[10]

These comments, again, send mixed messages. The man has "deficiencies" and yet Marlow "worried" about the man with whom he felt "a subtle bond."

Further evidence of what seems to be selective reading on Achebe's part comes earlier in his article when he makes a rather blatant change in the text. According to Achebe, Marlow says, "What thrilled you was just the thought of their humanity—like yours. Ugly" (Achebe, 316). In fact, what Marlow says is "...what thrilled you was just the thought of your remote kinship with the wild and passionate uproar. Ugly." Achebe repeats his misquotation later in his essay. The change in language is significant, especially in view of the fact that Conrad was so careful in his choice of words. In Achebe's version the idea of shared kinship is missing, despite the fact that it is central to the novel's purpose.

Achebe's strongest argument, however, is his insistence that Conrad's "bloody racism" results in a novel that cannot be considered "great" because it "sets people against people," and because "poetry should be on the side of man's deliverance and not his enslavement" (320). Achebe supports this contention with Marlow's description of the incident with the fireman. But, as we have seen, that incident is anything but one-sided. Marlow's feelings toward the fireman exhibit racist antipathy alongside a gradual awareness of a common human bond—"a claim of distant kinship." But this is not enough for Achebe, who wants Conrad to step forward and declare himself on the side of the brotherhood of mankind. This declaration, however, would jettison the aesthetic elements and reduce the novel to a pamphlet. If such a reduction were to occur, and I would insist it does not, then the novel would indeed fail as a work of art—not because we do or do not agree with its message, but because it would be propaganda. Such a reduction can only occur, however, if the reader mistakes part for whole. Achebe does precisely this: he reads through a pre-ground lens that eliminates alternative ways of seeing and filters out those elements of ambiguity that are essential to the novel as a work of art.

In this regard, one wonders why Achebe seems to miss Marlow's attitude toward the cannibals. Achebe barely mentions them and yet they form a most interesting contrast to the ridiculous Europeans, and Marlow's attitude toward them weakens Achebe's charge that the novel is "racist." Their very silence is a strength in the midst of the silly babble spoken by the Europeans. Furthermore, Marlow admires their "restraint," especially when he tosses the body of the dead helmsman overboard. These men haven't eaten solid food for weeks. Marlow describes his own reaction at some length:

> Yes, I looked at them as you would on any human being, with a curiosity of their impulses, motives, capacities, weaknesses, when brought to the test of an inexorable physical necessity. Restraint! What possible restraint? Was it superstition, disgust, patience, fear—or some kind of primitive honor? No fear can stand up to hunger, no patience can wear it out, disgust simply does not exist where hunger is; and as to superstition, beliefs, and what you may call principles, they are less than chaff in a breeze. Don't you know the devilry of lingering starvation, its exasperating torment, its black thoughts, its somber and brooding ferocity? Well, I do. It takes a man all his inborn strength to fight hunger properly... Restraint! I would just as soon have expected restraint from a hyena prowling among the corpses of a battlefield. But there was the fact facing me....[11]

What we find here is a grudging admiration on Marlow's part mixed inextricably with the contempt reflected in the simile involving the hyena prowling among corpses. The thing to note, however, is precisely the mixture of these elements. This is evidence of the poetic imagination at work, and of the conflict within the poet's mind that I alluded to earlier. After all, the cannibals show the very quality that Kurtz (even Kurtz!) fails to exhibit.

I noted earlier that one thing Marlow admires about civilization is its promotion of restraint. Self-restraint, coupled with enlightenment, is essential to balance the greed and ugliness which surround him. As Marlow puts it, "What redeems it is the idea only. An idea at the back of it; not a sentimental pretense, but an idea; and an unselfish belief in the idea...."[12] And yet, in the end, it is a group of cannibals who exhibit restraint. There is no explanation for it. It makes no sense to him: it challenges all his preconceptions. But there it was "facing" Marlow stubbornly. Such ambivalence and uncertainty about civilization and about racial "superiority" or "inferiority" weakens Achebe's case against Conrad's novel and leads me to insist that it is, indeed, a great piece of literature, worthy of being read and taken seriously.

Achebe's claim, if allowed, has serious consequences for both aesthetics and literary criticism. Achebe would have us criticize art using moral precepts. However, while I do not question Achebe's moral principles and might also prefer that all written works foster those principles, the issue of whether Conrad's novel can be considered "great" is not a moral question; it is a question of aesthetics. This is not to say that content is irrelevant, but that it is only a part of the whole. The question is not one of the message and whether we approve of it; the question is whether the work forms a substantial whole, whether it succeeds as a work of art.

In the end, *Heart of Darkness* does not foster any particular message, racist or otherwise. Most assuredly it does not "call into question" the "very humanity of black people." Its descriptions of the natives are conflicting, at times favorable and at times stereotypical; it is written not to arouse hatred or suspicion between the races, but, rather, to hold the reader's attention and, perhaps, to unsettle his or her convictions and prejudices. As a work of art, it requires full reader attention and imaginative involvement and effects a panoply of emotions both strong and weak, positive and negative. Clearly, Conrad, the novelist, wanted his readers to enter a world of his making, a world filled with uncertainties, and to make those uncertainties their own. Bits and pieces of what Conrad said are much too thickly enmeshed in the manner of their saying to be yanked out and treated on their own: too much is left behind in the process. In his criticism of this novel, Achebe has reached into the patient's body, removed a vital organ, raised it in triumph, and shouted, "Behold, the patient is dead!" It will not do.

If Achebe's case against Conrad had been successful, it would constitute a good reason not only to regard the book in a lesser light, but perhaps to avoid it altogether. This raises a deeper question that is germane to our present discussion and which I have so far ignored: what makes a novel a "racist" novel?

There would seem to be several possible answers to this question:

(1) The author exhibits racist attitudes in describing the characters within the novel.

(2) The narrator exhibits racist attitudes in the things he or she says in the novel.

(3) The novel condones racism.

(4) The novel promotes racism.

Achebe never makes it quite clear which of the above claims he is making against Conrad. It seems, though, that he is maintaining both (1) and (3), and possibly (4) as well. I have tried to show that (1) collapses into (2) in Conrad's novel, because we cannot determine exactly what the author's own private attitudes are from reading the novel: they seem ambivalent. However, (2) is not serious, because the narrator may present *any* point of view as a matter of literary license. How hamstrung writers would be if their characters could exhibit no socially unacceptable attitudes! Imagine, as David Lodge has,

> an intellectual environment in which it is frowned upon or
> expressly forbidden to say or write anything that might offend

an individual's or a group's values, self-esteem, sense of cultural
and ethnic identity, religious beliefs, or special interests. [Such
an environment] is not one in which the budding literary
imagination is likely to flourish. Important writers are often
rebellious, arrogant, irreverent, even outrageous.... Political correctness encourages caution, parochialism, and self-censorship.[13]

A novel is not "racist," however, even if (3) is true, though
we might have some doubts about such a book. But if (4) could
be shown, we would have a serious case to make against a
novel. In *Heart of Darkness* (3) is doubtful (because of the
narrator's own ambivalence within the novel itself) and I would
argue that (4) is almost certainly not the case. Neither the narrator nor the author can be said to be "racist," and in neither
case does the novel "promote" racism, despite Achebe's claim
that Conrad attempts to "dehumanize" Africans.

As I suggested in the previous chapter, however, Oscar
Wilde goes too far in thinking that the "message" contained in
fiction simply does not matter one way or the other. If the
message the novel imparts is strong enough to overpower the
aesthetic elements, there might be cause for alarm. But if the
aesthetic elements can hold out, and the message is only one
of many, Wilde is certainly correct in taking a purist stand. The
claim would have to be argued on a case-by-case basis. In this
case, the aesthetic elements are powerful, and Conrad's novel
is truly a great work of art.

What does this have to do with education and enabling young people to think for themselves? If I am correct about the nature and purpose of education, it is critical that young people have novels precisely like Conrad's, which pin them down between conflicting loyalties and force them to think their way through two, or even three, sides of complex issues.

If students are fed novels that are clearly ideological (racist, which we do not approve of, or feminist, which presumably we do), then they will take away from the novel precisely what the author intends. Further, if those attitudes are reinforced by the professor in the classroom, the student cannot possibly be expected to think for himself. This is what I meant earlier when I said that "great" novels are "foolproof" (which I qualified because of readers, and teachers, such as Achebe). What great novels do is to confront readers with conflicting points of view and force them to think their way out, as it were, even if the professor happens to promote one particular interpretation. That is to say, if a teacher tried to teach *Heart of Darkness* as a racist novel, the student should be able to see for himself that there are serious doubts about this claim, if he is willing and able to engage the novel on its own terms.

If, on the other hand, we combine a clearly ideological novel such as Alice Walker's *Meridian,* or even Achebe's *Things Fall Apart,* with a teacher who is zealous about the message pounded home in the novels (even if we happen to agree with the message), we have a formula for educational failure. The result of such an approach is a student who merely parrots the teacher's, or the author's, point of view. This will not necessarily happen in the context of four years of college courses, because other points of view will be presented to the student over the course of time in different courses taught by different professors. But students sometimes take three or four courses with the same professor, and academic departments are becoming increasingly homogeneous; this can lead to a type of imprinting if the student hears the same message repeatedly. Clearly, this situation is antithetical to intellectual freedom, which is why the question of what students read is as important as how the readings are taught.

Chapter V

CITIZENSHIP IN A WORLD
OF DIFFERENCE

"I sit with Shakespeare and he winces not. Across the color line I walk arm and arm with Balzac and Dumas, where smiling men and welcoming women glide in gilded halls. From out of the caves of the evening that swing between the strong-limbed earth and the tracery of the stars, I summon Aristotle and Aurelius and what soul I will, and they come all graciously with no scorn or condescension. So, wed with truth, I dwell above the veil." —W. E. B. Du Bois

Cultural pluralism is inexorable. As a movement toward increasing concerns over culture and gender differences and the uniqueness of particular perspectives it will only get stronger. But it is a mixed blessing. To the extent that it makes us aware of different ways of regarding our world and awakens us to our own cultural bias, crusty dogmas, smugness, and puffery, the movement is long overdue. But there are zealots who seek to control the movement and encircle it with high walls of intolerance; they would turn cultural difference into an idol and create a parareligious orthodoxy whose critics are condemned to Dante's eighth circle of Hell. This arm of the movement I shall call "militant multiculturalism," for it is a form of cultural pluralism that has been described by a recent author as "a movement that seeks to maintain the boundaries that divide hereditary groups and to promote solidarity within those groups...regardless of what individual members of these groups may desire.... [Their] target is the transethnic principles of voluntary pluralism and individual liberty."[1]

In this form, the movement is relativist, reductionist, and intolerant—qualities usually associated with belief groups rather than with intellectual or scientific communities. Accordingly, this movement bears close scrutiny as it seeks to elbow its way to a place at the table of higher education, a table overcrowded and inadequate to feed those already craving nourishment.

Because of its inexorability, there is little point in questioning whether we should continue to move in the direction of cultural pluralism, or "diversity" as it is sometimes called. So I shall not do so. Rather, I shall focus instead on some of the dangers that lurk at the center of militant multiculturalism—especially as they affect liberal education.

To begin with, we need to keep in mind that the purpose of liberal education is to allow young people to achieve positive freedom; that is, to take possession of their own minds. This purpose centers on a need that is common to all people at all times, because to the extent to which it is possible for them to be so, all people everywhere need to be free. This is the original meaning of the liberal arts: they liberate the autonomous human agent within each of us.

For the Greeks, of course, this goal required involvement in the *polis* or, as Aristotle would have it, the exercise of civic virtue. What is of chief interest to us today about this somewhat archaic notion is that education was regarded as the vehicle by which young people became law-abiding members of a human group. The *polis* was at once a political, intellectual, and moral community in which participation was essential if people were to become fully human. It was necessary for those who would practice civic virtue to develop the skills that might enable them to become full-fledged members of their community: skills of speaking, writing, listening, reasoning, and figuring. Civic virtue meant the ability to obey and to make laws, and two essential requirements were to be male and to own property. We now realize how narrow Aristotle's vision was on this issue, and, from our contemporary perspective, "people" includes all human beings, and the community of which we are a part is no longer the *polis,* it is the world. Citizenship now means membership in the world community. This notion of "membership" requires clarification.

People become members of athletic teams by joining and showing their willingness to subordinate their individual will to the success of the team. As coaches are fond of saying, "There's no 'I' in team!" Trite though this is, it is true, and it's not a bad analogy for our present purpose. The important thing to notice is that individuals benefit when they show a willingness to make the success of the team their primary focus by subordinating their particular will to the good of the group. This is precisely what citizenship involves, as Rousseau showed in his *Social Contract*.

In a just political society, individual citizens realize that the common good is synonymous with their own individual good. What benefits all benefits each. That is, the citizen, as a member of the political community, wills to do what is best for all, which at the same time is what is in that individual's long-term self-interest. I hasten to note that this adage is contrary to ethical egoism as it is found in the writings of many popular psychologists. I am not contending that if each of us follows short-term self-interest an "invisible hand" will bring about social justice. Nor am I maintaining, like Carl Rogers, that if each of us pursues "self-actualization" the result will be a harmony of selves. This view is untenable, and (if I may say so) psychologically naive. The key concept here is *enlightened* self-interest, and enlightenment requires thought, discipline, and self-denial. If educated persons pursued enlightened self-interest, harmony would indeed result, because what is good for all is good for each—the common good is the goal of citizenship in the end, and education is the necessary means to that end.

Many of us have problems with this notion in our present political setting, however, because the machinations of the government seem to be unrelated to our individual wills: the common good seems to be the farthest thing from the minds of professional politicians and policy makers. But as citizens we are showing signs of our own myopia as well: we want what *we* want and we tend to confuse freedom with independence, when in fact freedom is a function of dependence upon things not of our own making. Positive freedom is a function of dependence upon principles that inform our thinking and a commitment to truth which stands outside ourselves and directs our inquiry.

Positive freedom is self-determination, the willing of reasonable strictures and codes. In the present context, it appears as "self-governance," and the phrase exposes the two sides of positive freedom, one private and the other public. The public side encompasses the "political" life of the human animal (as the term "politics" is properly used) and it is almost totally ignored in current discussions of the nature and purpose of education. Negative freedom is personal freedom, my choice, not yours; positive freedom is public freedom—what Montaigne called "political freedom," the freedom that makes it possible "to do what we ought to will." The first fosters competition and promotes self-interest, while the second fosters cooperation and reasonable compromise. The lack of concern for positive freedom in our schools has created a vacuum into which we have thrust the narrow, self-directed notion of negative liberty which, at times, is mere license. As Scott Buchanan has said, our "exclusive addiction to individual liberty of choice, conditioned by competitive economy and industry and their temptation to build wealth and power, [has] forced the competitive system into education, where the young are thus thrown back into the occupations of private individuals without the benefit of the common concern for public happiness."[2]

The political side is especially important in a democracy, where the goal of positive freedom involves citizenship, or what Aristotle called "civic virtue." Citizens in a democracy must work and find pleasure, but they must also be free agents: they must be able to imagine and to read and think critically, write clearly, listen carefully, argue cogently, choose wisely, and figure accurately. Moreover, they must also know how the system works and how to make certain that it fosters "the common good." Positive freedom is a goal that involves the proper understanding of one's relationship to others. That is to say, one does not achieve freedom at another's expense, but only as a member of a community of free persons.

This point may be illustrated with an example. Let us suppose that Maynard is a 53-year-old widower with no children. Maynard insists that he should pay no property taxes since he is childless and will never send anyone to public school. Now he could exercise his negative freedom and not pay his property taxes—if he is willing to suffer the consequences. But if Maynard thinks about what he *ought* to do (as Montaigne would have it), he would pay his taxes, since support of public education (properly pursued) is fundamental to a healthy democratic society. It is not a sufficient condition for a healthy democracy, but it is, most assuredly, a necessary one.

If Maynard exercises his positive freedom, there is no conflict between what he wants to do and what he ought to do, because taxes benefit each of us by benefiting all of us; Maynard, knowing this, chooses to do the right thing. In this case, as is typical, the "right thing" is not a vague philosophical concept; it is simply what is in Maynard's long-term self-interest. As noted in a previous chapter, Rousseau expressed this point somewhat paradoxically by saying that, in these cases, people such as Maynard are "forced to be free"; that is, they do what they really want to do, though not necessarily what they think they want to do. Our short-term self-interest does not always accord with our long-term self-interest. We can see this more clearly if we examine in greater detail what we must imagine to have gone on in Maynard's mind as he deliberated whether to pay his taxes. In the process of probing into this matter more deeply, we will come to a clearer understanding of positive freedom as it affects citizenship.

I shall employ several rather simple examples. Their simplicity must not obscure the fact that important differences are being indicated.

EXAMPLE #1: A: "Pay your property taxes."

Maynard pays his taxes.

EXAMPLE #2: A: "Pay your property taxes."

Maynard: "Why?"

A: "Because I say so."

Maynard pays his taxes.

EXAMPLE #3: A: "Pay your property taxes."

Maynard: "Why?"

A: "Because it is the law."

Maynard pays his taxes.

EXAMPLE #4: A: "Pay your property taxes."

Maynard: "Why?"

A: "Because it is the right thing to do."

Maynard pays his taxes.

In all of these cases, Maynard does what is demanded of him: he pays his taxes. But in each case he does so for a different reason. It is this difference that is basic to a proper understanding of positive freedom.

In Example #1, Maynard simply obeys; his obedience is passive—it may result from reflex, from habit, because Maynard is preoccupied with other thoughts, or for a host of other reasons. But it does not involve a process of deliberation. Maynard does not *internalize* the law here. He does not make it a principle of his own action, but simply acts without reflecting on the question of why it is that he acts. This is a paradigm case of passive decision making, and it is commonplace. In the other three cases, however, at least some reflection is involved, as can be seen by the occurrence of the question "Why?" In the second example, however, Maynard's obedience may also be passive, since it follows from, let us say, his fear of "A," desire of reward from "A," fear of punishment (sanction), or other similar factors—with no regard for law as such. If, in this second example, Maynard obeys "A" out of respect for "A" (let us say that "A" is a person in a position of authority), then Maynard's obedience might appear to be active, if he were to adopt the maxim: "One ought always to obey persons in positions of authority." The same reasoning might also seem to apply in the third example. But the fourth case is the clearest of all.

The important thing to suppose here is that in saying that paying his taxes is "the right thing to do," "A" can provide reasons for this claim, or Maynard can determine for himself that the reasoning is sound. If neither of these is the case, Maynard must accept this claim on faith and the example becomes a special case of Example #2, and nothing else. If paying his taxes is the right thing to do, that is, if it will in fact promote Maynard's best interest and Maynard makes this determination, then he can internalize the law and act, because he knows that it is the right thing to do; as Spinoza would have it, his action will mesh with his "own true advantage." That is to say, his obedience to law is positively free. This presupposes that the reasons for obeying the law are good reasons—they must be capable of persuading a person of critical intelligence, or what Chaim Perelman called "the Universal Audience," which "refers, of course, not to an experimentally proven fact, but to a universality and a unanimity imagined by the speaker, to the agreement of an audience which should be universal, since, for legitimate reasons, we need not take into consideration those which are not a part of it.... The agreement of a universal audience is thus a matter, not of fact, but of right."[3]

If the reasons for obedience to the tax laws are not good reasons, then Maynard cannot internalize the reasons for paying his property taxes and make them the principles of his own right action. He cannot obey freely in this case. If, on the other hand, Maynard can perform this transposition, then he can obey this law freely. *He is free if he does what is right because it is right and he knows it to be right.*

The critical issue here is how Maynard relates to the law at the moment he is faced with a decision to obey or not to obey the law. The question is: can the person make the law a principle or rule for his own self-determined act? He can do so if, and only if, he determines that the law is in his own long-term self-interest; it must be a just law: what he does must be "the right thing."

Positive freedom is therefore a function of knowledge and our ability to assimilate that knowledge and bring it to bear on concrete decisions. This is why education is so important. If the individual knows that a law is in accordance with his "own true advantage," and elects to obey it accordingly, then he is free. If he does not know, or if the law is not in his long-term self-interest, or if he obeys unthinkingly, then he does not act freely.

In the present context, paying property taxes is Maynard's "own true advantage," for we must assume that he wants to live in a healthy democracy, whether or not he has children. And if Maynard considers his own long-term self-interest, he will acknowledge that he is better off in a democracy in which the young are educated than he is in one in which they are not. Since Maynard wants his country to be healthy, he will pay the taxes.

This argument rests on two assumptions, of course. On the one hand, it assumes that the schools are educating the young, which, as things now stand, is doubtful. On the other hand, and more importantly for our present purposes, it also assumes that there is one (and only one) "right" thing to do in a given case. This second assumption is not widely accepted in our relativistic age, but it requires only that there *be* a right thing, not that Maynard (or anyone else) knows what that one thing is. The determination is dialectical and open-ended at that. The best we can do is to examine the grounds for the decision to pay or not to pay the taxes, as we did above, and consider carefully which one seems to be the more reasonable option, which is to say the option that would persuade the Universal Audience. This does not guarantee certainty, but it assures us that the actions we take will be rationally grounded. In principle, this point seems clear, but in fact it is difficult to determine in a given case what is the "right" thing to do. Difficult, but not impossible.

Consider another example. Sally and Fred want to buy a new car. Sally wants a car that is economical and safe and one that will also last a long time. Fred wants an SUV, because he thinks it combines luxury and comfort with increased safety. Given that Sally and Fred live in Atlanta, it is not clear why they would need a four-wheel-drive vehicle, especially since neither of them has the desire to drive "off-road." Given also that SUVs guzzle gasoline, pollute the environment, contribute to global warming, and may lose their resale value quickly, Fred's case seems weak, indeed.

Note that these reasons, if correct, are "good reasons," in that they will persuade the Universal Audience. They may not persuade Fred, but that is immaterial. Good reasons are reasons everyone *should* find persuasive; that we do not do so may be the result of psychological factors that advertisers understand better than we. This is where liberal education comes in, since, as I have said, it puts us into a position to separate reasons we cannot find fault with (good reasons) from reasons we merely find comfortable. The reasons against buying the SUV may not be comfortable to Fred, but they are good reasons if they can withstand scrutiny. This would seem to be the heart of the Socratic *maieutic*, which proposes and then disposes of intellectually weak reasons, and it may be the best we can do in the hurly-burly of the everyday world.

It is true that SUVs are safer than other cars in collisions; and if Fred and Sally lived in a cold climate and had to deal with snow and ice, Fred's case would be stronger. But as it stands, in this instance the "right" thing to do is to buy the car Sally has her eye on. Whether Sally and Fred do this, of course, depends on a myriad of nonrational factors, but those factors do not affect the argument itself: the reasonable thing, the course of action that appears to be in Sally's and Fred's best interest, is to pass on the SUV—unless better reasons are forthcoming.

This example shows how free choices come about, and it shows how an apparently personal decision can also be a public one. The fact that more than half the cars now bought are SUVs and that they adversely affect the environment and waste a limited resource (oil) leads one to suspect that many people do not act freely—specifically, that they do not consider the consequences of their actions or consider their own long-term self-interest. Presumably, this is what Rousseau meant when he opened his *Social Contract* with the enigmatic line, "Men are born free but are everywhere in chains."[4]

This suggestion is reinforced by the data that show, in the political realm, that the vast majority of Americans do not know who their two senators are and cannot name a single policy either senator stands for. Furthermore, in a recent poll, upon being confronted by passages from the Declaration of Independence, a majority thought it was a "communist" document! Clearly, such people cannot exercise their civic responsibilities in a reasonable and informed manner: they are not free, they are enslaved by the goddess Whimsy and their own ignorance.

Positive political freedom requires that people be able to determine in a given case whether a course of action is to their "own true advantage." Such a determination requires, minimally, that people be sufficiently well informed and be able to distinguish between their short-term and long-term self-interests.

Citizenship thus understood requires the intellectual skills that have always been fostered by the liberal arts. The point has nowhere been better stated than it was some thirty years ago by Scott Buchanan, who told us that "school is the traditional preparation for life, but it is also basic preparation for politics. In it there is the irrepressible attempt to raise reason from private to public concerns, to raise the art of bargaining for mutual private advantage to the art of deliberation for the common good, so that combats by force and threat may become subjects for common deliberation."[5]

Ironically, the demands of many postmodern thinkers are precisely designed to lead students to greater political responsibility through a heightened sense of social injustice. This goal cannot be reached, however, if teachers simply impose their own sense of injustice on their students, a point that is illustrated in a recent comment by Gerald Graff, who criticized the National Association of Scholars for fostering a return to the Great Books. He noted that young people cannot read Plato without knowing something about the injustices of a slave society. This is absurd, of course, since one can read Plato best by simply attending to what he has to say: concerns about the injustices prevalent in his culture (and our own) will come later with thought. Being told that Plato's society was unjust will not promote thought: reading what Plato has to say with an open mind will. That is the difference between education and indoctrination.

Clearly, the current demands on higher education to raise political consciousness and right past wrongs—demands that often come from within the academy itself—do little to clarify or provide focus. The academy cannot be all things to all people and if it continues to ignore its specific purpose—that which makes it unique among social institutions—it will do nothing well. This seems to be our present dilemma.

If we are to keep afloat in the maelstrom that threatens to drag us down, we must remain clear about what it is we are supposed to be doing, which is to educate young men and women for freedom. This will, among other things, prepare them for effective political involvement. Here it might be prudent to recall what Aristotle said about healthy political states. It still rings true and it is central to our present discussion.

The controlling idea of Aristotle's political philosophy was the notion that healthy states differ from unhealthy states in that the former concern themselves with the common good while the latter splinter into multiple concerns about particular goods—usually centered around the specific demands of particular citizens. Rousseau later called groups preoccupied with their own special concerns "cabals and factions" and warned that they obtrude between citizens and "The General Will." Alexis de Tocqueville later warned against this tendency toward "individualism,"

> which disposes each member of the community to sever himself from the mass of his fellows, and to draw himself apart with his family and his friends so that, after he has thus formed a small circle of his own, he willingly leaves society at large to itself.[6]

This is not to say that humans ought not be motivated by self-interest or that the Western ideal of individuality is wrong-headed. We should not confuse *individuality*, which involves pride in self and a healthy regard for one's own long-term self-interest, with *individualism,* which is simply the pursuit of short-term self-interest. To fault individuality would be absurd, and none of the writers I have mentioned does this, least of all Tocqueville, who joined Mill in warning against the "tyranny of the majority." What Aristotle, Rousseau, and Tocqueville meant was that our notion of self-interest must encompass the interest of others. Civic virtue redirects attention outward toward what is best for all. The practice of this sort of virtue requires the development of those skills of intellect and imagination that make it possible for us to envision consequences, recognize injustice, and develop reasonable plans of action as members of a group without which we are less than human. This is where citizenship and autonomy come together, and this is why citizenship properly understood should always be at the center of any discussion of the purpose of liberal education: a liberal education fosters those skills that make involvement in the community meaningful and productive for autonomous citizens. These citizens are precisely those who are able to act intelligently in fostering the common good, which they recognize as coincident with their own good.

As I have noted, however, citizenship today means world citizenship and not merely membership in small communities of like-minded people. World citizenship maintains at its center the notion of autonomous agents interacting with other members of the world community, whom they regard as their political equals and with whom they share equal rights. Though the idea of political equality remains central, the difference is that the community has now become all-inclusive. As Lisa Newton has said in another connection, "If citizenship is not a possibility, political equality is unintelligible." If, then, citizenship is undermined, "none of us is…a citizen, a bearer of rights—we are all petitioners for favors."[7]

The term "citizenship" was coined during the Enlightenment and it retains its eighteenth-century concern with the development of reason and respect for truth. It requires an ability to think critically and engage with others in dialogue in order to arrive at reasoned judgments to which we willingly submit. It is ironic, in this regard, that militant multiculturalism, which began as a protest for equality in the name of the rights of disenfranchised minorities, has degenerated into a repressive ideology that denies the reality of a shared human nature—an idea that for the past two centuries (at least) has grounded those very rights. They are, after all, *human* rights. If, however, we cannot function in this world as citizens, we are indeed, as Newton says, reduced to the status of "petitioners for favors." In such a world, there is no difference between reasoned judgment and personal opinion, truth is relative, communication is impossible, and force replaces dialogue as a means to adjudicate differences. Might, in such a world, does in fact make right.

Perhaps it has come to that. To some, my concern for resurrecting the concept of citizenship and refocusing attention on civic virtue is an exercise in futility: I am beating a dead horse with the collected works of Aristotle. But to others, the current demise of dialogue as a way of finding reasonable solutions to pressing human problems simply emphasizes the depth of our current malaise and our need to recall the purpose of liberal education.

Unfortunately, militant multiculturalism does not concern itself with resolving conflict reasonably or building a sense of community across cultural boundaries. Rather, it separates human cultures and subcultures by emphasizing their distinct vocabularies and particular world views. In fact, militant multiculturalism does regard each individual, culture, or subculture as a "petitioner for favors," a view that leads invariably toward confrontation and conflict. Such a view is distorted and partial. Anne Wortham has noted in this regard that

> Most of all, [militant multiculturalism] denies the proposition that persons from different backgrounds can be united by ideas and values that transcend the interests, beliefs, and norms of particular groups and subcultures. Instead of promoting intergroup relations based on such universal criteria as rationality, personal autonomy, and individual rights, [militant multiculturalism] affirms cultural particularism—the doctrine that persons belonging to different cultural groups should be treated differently.... The multicultural education movement's

efforts to impose "cultural diversity" on college and grade school curricula is fueled by just this particularism.[8]

The correct view, as I have already suggested, is a balanced one that allows for the truth buried at the center of multi-culturalism and, at the same time, stresses the fundamental sameness of all members of the human community. That view was expressed in the eighteenth century by Giambattista Vico, who coined the term "cultural pluralism." Vico acknowledged that differences among cultures are interesting, important, and occasionally ineluctable. At the same time, he insisted that understanding across cultural boundaries is possible because all humans share a common nature. The same point was made by the Japanese philosopher Kitaro Nishida, who said, "I think that insofar as we are humans with shared reason we necessarily think in the same way and seek things in the same way."[9] In education, this commonality must remain at the center of any discussion of purpose, since it is human freedom that education must seek to achieve—not the freedom of this or that particular political group.

Even before the current fuss over multiculturalism, higher education was confused about its purpose. If the battle over cultural pluralism does nothing else than force us to regroup and reconsider with great seriousness the question of what it is we are about, it will have turned out to be of immense benefit to higher education in America. If, however, we allow ourselves to be lulled into thinking that by simply changing the status quo and indulging every special interest we will somehow resuscitate a lifeless educational system and correct past errors in judgment, we are deluding ourselves. We can survive our current crisis only by recalling what the academy can do that no other social institution can do, and that is to free young minds from the captivity of impulse, passion, preoccupation with self, and ideological myopia. Once free, these minds can address the major issues of the day with the prospect of finding workable solutions. That is to say, education produces citizens. Citizenship, properly understood, has always been the proper goal of higher education, and it remains so today.

Chapter VI

THE LIBERAL ARTS AND
THE PUBLIC COLLEGE

"Only law can give us liberty." —Goethe

I have argued that the liberal arts ought to be the focus of educational theory and practice, because only through a liberal education can we hope to help young people achieve positive freedom. This is not only a personal goal, as we have seen, but a public goal as well. Private colleges have always taken the lead in defending the liberal arts against the assaults of unfriendly forces, but even they have lately felt, not only from without but also from within, enormous pressure to jettison "useless" courses for a more politically correct or practical curriculum.

Public colleges have felt these pressures to a greater extent than private colleges, however, and their record to date has not been as laudable as has that of the private colleges—

for obvious reasons. They survive only by competing to recruit new students, and without years of tradition and elaborate alumni networks they must therefore be more responsive to student demands. Furthermore, their constituency is the general public, who pay taxes and who demand immediate returns on their tax dollars. And, increasingly, individuals in the public sphere—legislators and business leaders, for example—feel called upon to dictate policy to public colleges, even to the point of curricular change.

These pressures operate to an extent on all colleges and universities, to be sure. But these pressures must not be allowed to turn them into training academies. Too much is at stake. We must recover the purpose of higher education, not only to enable young men and women to succeed in their careers, but to assist them to become free and to enable them to function as active citizens in this democracy and the world at large.

For the past fifty years, the public college has been in a unique position to play a vital role in the education of citizens. The question we must address in this chapter is whether the public college intends to play that role. Thus, our focus shifts, but the concern remains the same: how can we enable young people to become autonomous, effective agents concerned about the common good as well as their own?

This ideal of effective action is Aristotelian to the core and has been given renewed emphasis by such thinkers as J. Glen Gray and Hannah Arendt. The person whose activity is a result of deliberate choice is the person who is free, in the sense that he is in control of himself and, as much as possible, in control of the situation around him as well. The person of passion and ignorance on the other hand, is constantly overcome by his emotions and the surrounding world, and, like Oedipus, is subject to tragic miscues. Plato describes the passionate person well and at some length in the *Republic:*

> Knowledge, right principles, true thoughts are not at their post; and the place lies open to the assault of false and presumptuous notions. So he turns again to those lotus-eaters and now throws in his lot with them openly. If his family send reinforcements to the support of his thrifty instincts, the impostors who have seized the royal fortress shut the gates upon them, and will not even come to parlay with the fatherly counsels of individual friends. In the internal conflict they gain the day; modesty and self-control, dishonored and insulted as the weaknesses of an unmanly fool, are thrust out into exile; and the whole crew of unprofitable desires take a hand in banishing moderation and frugality, which, as they will have it, are nothing but churlish meanness. So they take possession of the soul which they have swept clean, as if purified for initiation into higher mysteries; and nothing remains but to marshal the great procession bringing home Insolence, Anarchy, Waste, and Impudence, those resplendent divinities crowned with garlands, whose praises they sing under flattering names: Insolence they call good breeding, Anarchy they call freedom, Waste they call

magnificence, and Impudence they call a manly spirit.... [This man's] life is subject to no order or constraint and he has no desire to change an existence which he calls pleasant, free, and happy. [1]

To avoid this, we must educate for freedom, help young people become persons of action in Aristotle's sense of this term. Such persons will be prepared for the problems of the future because they can think, speak, read, write, and figure. Not only will they perceive a problem where a problem truly exists, but they will also be able to act effectively, which involves a knowledge of both what is required and what is possible, together with a determination to take appropriate action. Effective action necessitates thought because it presupposes self-control, which is fundamentally rational. The training of young minds to reason, as I have argued, is the role played traditionally by the liberal arts.

The seven liberal arts mentioned in the first chapter have had a bewildering number and variety of offspring—many of whom bear little or no resemblance to their parents. Indeed, one could go through almost any college catalog at random and eliminate a large number of courses that have nothing whatever to do with a liberal education. This variety doubtless explains why so many administrators at so many colleges and universities have so much trouble organizing divisions, colleges, and schools. The fine arts are sometimes included with the liberal arts, and mathematics and the natural sciences are frequently separated from them—as they are from the "humanities," with which the liberal arts are often mistaken.

What all liberal subjects have in common, that which defines them, is that they all focus on theory rather than information, principles rather than facts (which, contrary to popular opinion, do not "speak for themselves"). They seek to engender intellectual discipline and respect for a reasoned approach to the facts, which enables us, perhaps, to explain and understand why the facts are as they are. A liberal arts education is the most "relevant" education a person can attain—to borrow a term recently become popular. The point has been well made by Richard Weigle:

> No curriculum and no individual course can anticipate the information and the special skills which a world in rapid flux may well require of any individual a decade after he has left the comfortable confines of the college campus. Instead, the best guarantee for the future is a well-disciplined and highly versatile mind which can function freely and effectively. Such a mind is capable of tackling new and unfamiliar problems; it can analyze situations and define alternatives; it distinguishes fact from propaganda; it is likely to make the right decisions; it can communicate with others clearly and persuasively; it has developed a degree of competency in both of the languages men use, the language of words and the language of numbers. Such a mind is best prepared to undertake the demands of a specific vocation or profession, to serve the state as citizen or

official, and to seek intelligent solutions to the vast and intricate problems which can never be resolved by demonstrations and picket lines. The acquisition of the intellectual skills would appear to be highly relevant activity.[2]

A liberal education, however, has frequently been dismissed as "elitist." That is, the claim has often been made that only a few can benefit from such a study. This claim rests on a denial of the supposition that all persons are capable of self-rule. Such a denial would seem to make a democratic society an impossibility. If we are to say that a liberal education is necessary for persons to achieve freedom, and that democracies are healthy only if their citizens are not mere subjects, then it follows that everyone must be offered the opportunity, at least, to receive a liberal education—or we must give up the ideal of democracy as a society of self-governed persons. Even if we grant the necessity of educating all citizens in a democracy, however, what reason is there to believe such a plan is even possible? In other words, can we meet the "elitist" objection head-on?

Robert Hutchins has argued with some eloquence in *The Learning Society* that "everybody has a mind and...the ability, aptitude and need to learn to use it." He insists that "liberal education is for everybody because everybody has a right to have his/her mind set free."[3] But the evidence he adduces to establish this claim is rather thin. He refers to the example of the Soviet Union, where compulsory schooling "demands that all pupils learn, between the ages of seven and fifteen, the elements of mathematics, physical and biological science, and at least one foreign language." He says that observers agree that "instruction in these subjects has succeeded." To use a distinction I made in the second chapter, however, this is an example of schooling, not education. All the Russian example shows is that people *can* learn more than they usually do—which is plausible, but not very helpful for our purpose. It does not show that all people can achieve freedom in the form of self-governance. In order to do this, one must be able to think, and thought is one of the most demanding activities humans can engage in. As Plato saw so clearly, "the only way to get the understanding [a person] needs is to work for it like a slave." Hutchins insists that this effort will be well spent:

> All this implies the habit of thinking and the capacity to think about the most important matters. This, in turn, implies the capacity to distinguish the important from the unimportant. It implies the development of critical standards of thought and action.[4]

The heart of Hutchins' argument that everyone can be liberally educated rests on the claim of the psychologist Jerome Bruner, who presents "the hypothesis that any subject can be taught effectively in some intellectually honest form to any child at any state of his development."[5] If Bruner is correct, it may be that all people can not only accumulate more information than they do, but also, as he puts it, "grasp the great issues, principles, and values that a society deems worthy of the continued concern of its members."[6] In a word, perhaps all persons can learn to free their minds. To be sure, it is their right, and a free society does demand that all citizens be capable of thoughtful deliberation on matters of mutual concern. There is, however, very little evidence that Bruner is correct. Bruner's hypothesis is just that: a hypothesis; and as such it has never been fully tested. For this to change, higher public education, "the public college," would have to radically alter its priorities and redirect its attention, since the vast majority of our students receive their degrees in public institutions. Will this occur? It would seem not. Should it occur? To the extent to which it is possible for all students to achieve freedom, almost certainly. Let us take a closer look.

Since the end of World War II, when public colleges and universities began to proliferate with massive infusions of federal monies, their doors have opened wide to large numbers of students of diverse abilities and backgrounds. As a result, these institutions have been placed in a unique position to establish the truth or falsity of Bruner's hypothesis. Unfortunately, it would appear that the public college has not risen to the challenge, despite the fact that as tax-supported institutions they have a special interest in educating citizens. What has stood in the way of the realization of this goal?

As I shall argue in Chapter 9, a liberal education requires a close relationship among the disciplines and among the faculty and students who teach and learn together. Students must see the relationship between specific courses of instruction and other disciplines, as well as each course's relationship to the goal of a liberal education. To undergraduate students and to the faculty who work with them, no academic discipline can be viewed as being of paramount importance. This is not to demean the disciplines, but simply to call attention to the need for a common focus within the undergraduate curriculum; emphasis ought to be placed on a carefully structured, integrated course of study in which the disciplines complement one another and do not compete for dominance. What is required of higher education, at least on the undergraduate level, is a commitment to the liberal arts on the part of the faculty, acknowledgment of a common concern, expenditure of effort on quality teaching, and cooperation.

Unfortunately, the major universities that form the backbone of American public higher education seldom emphasize undergraduate education. Their commitment is to research and graduate programs. Private colleges, which tend to be more selective and in a position to cooperate and to commit themselves to the ideal of liberal education, on the other hand, cannot escape the "elitist" charge. The smaller public institutions, then, would appear to be best suited to carry out our experiment; that is, to prove to what extent all persons are educable. This bright prospect begins to dim, however, as we consider that thus far there has been little or no commitment to the liberal arts on the part of the public colleges. The concern to this point has been to provide our economy with workers rather than to provide our polity with citizens, and these institutions have shown the same tendencies toward splintering and lack of cooperation among academic departments as their larger models.

This consideration raises the important and perplexing question of the practicability of the approach to higher education suggested above. Is it reasonable to expect that this sort of plan can ever be realized, as a matter of fact? We are on the brink of an abyss of idle speculation, from which vantage point we can see two options.

One option is for educational institutions, private and public, to continue to scramble to satisfy the demands of career-oriented undergraduates. This seems a meandering road that leads nowhere, though it is one well traveled. More to the point, it denies young people the opportunity to free their minds. The other option is to rethink the question of what it is that educational institutions, including public educational institutions, are supposed to do that no other institutions can do, and then proceed from there with renewed energy.

This is not to say that the people who run our colleges and universities should ignore the legitimate concerns of their students regarding future employment. But there are guidance counselors and placement services to deal with these concerns: they are not institutional concerns and should not dictate curricular matters. I can find no good argument to show that our institutions of higher learning ought to make employment or employability their primary focus. Indeed, given pressures from society, there is considerable risk of confusion of purpose and dissipation of energies. These social pressures result from a particular set of historical circumstances about which the academy must inform itself but to which it must not submit. Otherwise, higher education will never play the social and political role for which it is best suited.

Practically speaking, however, while students look forward to bleak employment prospects, colleges face declining enrollments. This situation has forced colleges and universities to become "trendy," scratching the latest social itch as they try to survive in a competitive atmosphere. One bright spot on the horizon is the growth of adult education, as those who never entered college or who dropped out along the way determine to get their degrees. Although it may arise for the wrong reasons, institutions of higher learning are already devising a rhetoric to support the theme "education for a lifetime." The theme is certainly a legitimate one, although one must expect the worst in the way of rationale. At any rate, a more mature student population must be viewed as a bright prospect for higher education, though the number of such students is not yet significant. Unfortunately, the programs that have been put in place thus far for adults returning to college are largely "career-oriented" programs designed to help students acquire job skills and become more upwardly mobile. These programs have little to do with education for freedom, and are thus disappointing.

In addition, public institutions of higher learning—both large and small—are burdened with considerations such as "streamlining" and "cost accounting" that have nothing to do with learning and often interfere with the higher purposes of the academy. Furthermore, public institutions have not traditionally taken a leadership role in education and have viewed themselves in an economic rather than a political context—as job-training centers rather than educational institutions. At the same time, they have had, and continue to have, a unique opportunity to play a vital political role because of the wide spectrum of students they attract—making them best suited to this task of all the institutions that constitute the modern educational establishment.

But the tendency in American public education has been in the opposite direction entirely. Indeed, public colleges and universities are forced to compete for students in an increasingly shallow pool of high school graduates and seem determined to out-do the technical "colleges" (as they are now sometimes called) in offering "career" opportunities. They have bought into the myths I debunked in Chapter 2 to an alarming extent, and the humanities, arts, and natural sciences play an increasingly marginal role as students queue up to enroll in practical courses that they think will guarantee them jobs when they graduate.

The data are sobering. Between 1966 and 1993, for example, the percentage of students receiving B.A.'s in the humanities dropped from 40 percent to 30 percent, while the percentage in the social sciences (which have "practical" benefits) rose slightly, from 15.5 percent to 15.8 percent. The remaining 55 percent of B.A.'s, we must assume, have been issued in the natural sciences, fine arts, computer science, business, and education. These figures are for "more selective" liberal arts colleges (as determined by the Carnegie Commission in 1987).[7] But in the "less selective" liberal arts colleges, among which we would find virtually all of the public liberal arts colleges, the figures are even more disturbing. Degrees in the humanities dropped in this period from 26 percent to 10 percent. The specific disciplines included in these figures are English, foreign language, history, philosophy, and religion. The natural sciences are not much better off, dropping from 11.6 percent to 6.8 percent in all colleges and universities, including research universities.[8]

Thus, 83 percent of the students currently graduating from public colleges are completing majors in job-related fields rather than in the humanities and natural sciences. Louis Menand thinks much of this decline in popularity results from what he calls the "self-referentiality" of these academic subjects, chiefly in the humanities, which "makes what professors do the subject of what professors do." He adds that "it is hard to see, in a period of aggravated cost-consciousness, how it will be possible to sell the notion that what students and taxpayers are paying for is not knowledge, but rather debates among people who adhere to different interpretations but who cannot even agree on what counts as grounds for deciding on those interpretations." "If opinion is always contingent," Menand asks, "why should we subsidize professionals to produce it?"[9]

Allan Bloom put it otherwise when he said,

> The professors of humanities are in an impossible situation and do not believe in themselves or what they do. Like it or not, they are essentially involved with interpreting old books, preserving what we call tradition in a democratic society where tradition is not privileged. They are partisans of the leisured and beautiful in a place where evident utility is the only passport. Their realm is the always and the contemplative, in a setting that demands only the here and now and the active....[10]

Whatever the explanation, the data show that students are "opting out" of liberal studies to pursue studies that will lead them directly to good jobs. And the colleges and universities have made major adjustments in staffing and curricula to meet those demands.

Why is this cause for concern? Why should anyone care if students prefer computer science to philosophy or marketing to literature? For one thing, these are not careers, strictly speaking, but jobs. A job is simply something one does in order to make a living, something one "goes to" in order to make enough money to spend his or her free time pleasantly. A career is something in which one can continue to grow and develop and where one can find a degree of personal satisfaction. Data have shown that persons will change jobs at least five times before they reach the age of forty—often more frequently than that. Persons who choose a "career" at twenty usually experience disenchantment and want "more out of life." Frequently, however, those choices they made early on have squeezed them into narrow channels from which there is no escape. Instead of a broad-based education that trains the mind to be adaptable and grow, they find themselves with intellectual blinders firmly fixed and unable to see to either side. So, from the students' perspective, narrow specialization in restricted "career" fields is often a blunder of monumental proportions. It leaves many of the employed dissatisfied, reduces the options available to the unemployed to retrain themselves, and provides little sense of meaning to life outside of work. The result often is confusion and depression upon retirement.

From the perspective of our democratic society, of course, the consequences of the present trend are grave indeed. Young people narrowly trained to be computer programmers, book-keepers, managers, or marketing experts cannot be expected to function as free and active citizens who are capable of making informed choices in the political arena. They will, for the most part, "buy into" the latest fashion, be attracted by glitz, and find themselves unable to distinguish between self-interest and the real needs of society. They will be unable, in Scott Buchanan's words, "to raise reason from private to public concerns, to raise the acts of bargaining for mutual advantage to the art of deliberation for the common good."[11] Such a world is not one in which most of us would choose to live; it is a world in which civilized dialogue has ceased to function and in which we become, indeed, "petitioners for favors."

But the public college seems reluctant to respond to the challenge laid at its door in the form of a wonderfully hetero-geneous group of potential citizens. Even granting that some of these students do not want or perhaps could not benefit from a liberal education, it is a mistake to deny them the opportunity. As things now stand, whatever hope we have that future citizens will be well educated will have to find its source in the selective, private, small residential colleges and universities willing to commit themselves to learning rather than research. These institutions are the ones at present that are in a position to dictate curriculum rather than to merely respond to the latest trend, whether they do so or not. Unfortunately, this means that our democratic society will continue on whatever course is dictated by special interests, "cabals and factions," without meaningful participation on the part of an educated citizenry, the bulk of whom will have attended one of our public colleges, and who will feel increasingly estranged from a process they cannot fathom.[12]

Chapter VII

CAN VIRTUE BE TAUGHT?

"Education is what remains after the information that has been taught has been forgotten."
—Robert Hutchins

To this point I have expressed concern that many of our educational institutions are squandering their opportunity to educate young persons for freedom and active world citizenship. This is a serious concern, not only from the perspective of young persons, who usually don't know what they have forfeited, but also from the perspective of the political body, which consequently becomes increasingly remote from the citizens it seeks to serve. I have made the claim that the primary reason this has occurred is a confusion on the part of those who claim to educate about what it is they do. Part of this is due to the various demands placed on educational institutions which have nothing whatever to do with their central purpose. One such demand is that the schools teach the young to be "virtuous." But, prescinding for the moment from considering whether this is desirable, is teaching virtue even possible?

Plato's *Meno* starts with a barrage of outrageous questions put to Socrates by the brash and impatient young man for whom the dialogue is named: "Can you tell me, Socrates, is human excellence (*arete*) something teachable? Or, if not teachable, is it something to be acquired by training? Or, if it cannot be acquired either by training or by teaching, does it accrue to me at birth or in some other way?" As we might predict, Socrates tosses the questions back to Meno instead of trying to answer any of them. Then, in his own meandering way, Socrates follows Meno to the rather tentative conclusion that if we could find teachers of "human excellence," or virtue, we might be able to teach it, but, as we cannot find teachers, virtue cannot be taught.

All of this seems to have been lost on those who currently insist that our educational institutions teach virtue—whether or not we can find anyone capable of teaching it. In this regard, the Rev. Theodore Hesburgh, former president of the University of Notre Dame, made an uncharacteristically foolish comment during the Watergate scandal some years ago. Noting that the men who committed the Watergate break-in were lawyers and therefore (presumably) educated men, he suggested that this incident exposed the basic failure of our educational system. That is to say, our educational systems failed because they did not succeed in teaching these particular burglars to be virtuous. The irony of this comment coming from a man of the cloth should not have been lost on anyone, but I shall pass over it to note some other oddities about the remark and the sense of outrage that is directed against institutions of education in general and institutions of higher education in particular because of their failure to teach virtue.

To begin with, Father Hesburgh assumes that there is an inherent connection between schooling and education, which is questionable, as I showed in the second chapter. Unfortunately, there seems to be little correlation between how much time one spends in school and the level of education one actually receives. Everything depends on the school and what a person does while there. But more importantly, the suggestion that education should have anything whatever to do with virtue is a claim that needs to be argued, especially in light of Socrates' response to Meno.

As in the case of Plato's dialogue, we must begin with an examination of just what virtue is. Unlike Meno, we are fortunate to have Aristotle to assist us, and he has told us that "human excellence" is fundamentally a matter of character. Once character has been formed, we can begin to discuss what he calls "intellectual virtue," which is peculiar to humans but impossible without sound character. This latter quality is called "moral virtue" by Aristotle, and it is primarily a matter of conditioning—what Aristotle calls "habit" or "disposition" (*ethos*). Moral virtue is learned by repetition; intellectual virtue can be taught and is the appropriate concern of the schools. Moral virtue is acquired, if it is acquired at all, at a very early age. And while it is not clear just how "early" this age is, we might recall Plato's abortive attempts to educate Dion's son in Syracuse. These repeated attempts failed because the young man was already vain, undisciplined, and self-absorbed by the time Plato started to work with him. The last attempt nearly cost Plato his life and later, at the Academy, the story must have made a powerful impression on Plato's pupil Aristotle. In addition, Aristotle had a number of other examples of bright and promising young men gone awry—notably Alcibiades, for whom not even the friendship of Socrates could be a palliative.

We now know, from the findings of psychologists, that what Aristotle called "moral virtue," or "character," is formed quite early. Freud thought it was formed by the time a child is five. This would suggest that by the time young people start their formal schooling, or very soon thereafter, their character is already essentially formed. What does this mean? Specifically, what implications does it have as far as the role of education and its relationship to building sound character are concerned? To be sure, there is a popular assumption, reflected in Father Hesburgh's comment, that educated people ought to be good people. But is there any reason to assume any connection whatever between sound character and sound education? More to the point, is there any good reason to require that college students take certain kinds of courses—ethics, for example—on the grounds that those courses will help make those students better people? Can we make sense of the claim that virtue is teachable and that our colleges should be producing people who are better for having spent roughly four years there? We should probably suspect from some of Socrates' hints that much of our thinking is wrongheaded—not all of it, but much of it. To clarify things a bit, let us recall some of the things Aristotle said on the same subject.

The bulk of the second book of *The Nicomachean Ethics* deals with the doctrine of "the mean" and contains a careful analysis of the process of deliberation. These topics have received considerable attention over the years, with good reason, but there are several chapters at the beginning of the second book that are of considerable interest as well. It is in those chapters that Aristotle spells out his idea of the importance of early habit formation: the basis of moral virtue, or character. Sound moral character is formed "right from early youth," as Plato says, and arises out of the disposition to "find pleasure or pain in the right things." In modern dress, the doctrine seems entirely plausible. If a parent wants his or her child to be considerate, honest, and trustworthy, then that parent will encourage the child to practice activities generally recognized as considerate, honest, and trustworthy and make sure the child takes pleasure in those activities—and not in their opposites. In contemporary terms, then, Aristotle seems to be talking about positive and negative reinforcement. We reward "right actions" so the child will take pleasure in those actions, and we punish wrong actions so the child will find them unpleasant. What is important, however, is not the label we place on this sort of training, but the insight that if we want children to become considerate, honest, and trustworthy, we will see to it that they take pleasure in those actions. The result will be that those kinds of actions become a matter of habit or disposition. As the child grows older, he will incline toward right actions and away from wrong actions. This is true of all virtuous actions: repetition and reward will bring about the disposition to be virtuous. Aristotle is recognizing here the important psychological fact that unless a person *wants* to be a good person— that is, unless he takes pleasure in right actions—he will not be one. Virtue, at this level, has more to do with willing than it does with thinking.

The fact that Aristotle's emphasis on practical reasoning has received the lion's share of attention over the years should not blind us to this fundamental insight, which forms one of the cornerstones of his ethical system: without sound moral character, no amount of reasoning will be effective. Unless a person finds honesty, reliability, and consideration of others to be pleasurable, no syllogism will ever cause that person to act in an honest, reliable, or considerate manner. For Aristotle, deliberation has to do with means, not ends. If one wants to be healthy, one will exercise. A practical syllogism will lead straight to this conclusion. But unless one wants to be healthy (because he realizes that this, in turn, will help make him happy), one will never do a single push-up or jog a step. Similarly, unless one is disposed to be kind and considerate to others, he will never select the appropriate means to other-directed actions. Everything depends upon disposition or character: the kind of person one becomes is determined by whether one takes "pleasure in the right things."

In the end, then, virtuous actions require sound moral character, and, as one grows in experience, he also requires the ability to deliberate and choose. At this stage, Aristotle shifts focus to discuss "intellectual virtue" (*nous*), which is that virtue that is peculiar to humans and that would constitute a major part of the education a young person receives as he or she matures. Though it may be difficult in a particular case to tell precisely where moral virtue leaves off and intellectual virtue begins, the latter has to do with the development of the thought process—specifically, the development of reason and "practical wisdom." It has to do with choice and the "mean relative to us."

We must guard against the mistake of supposing that Aristotle, or anyone else who adopts his scheme, regards moral and intellectual virtue as discrete entities—compartments of the human psyche, as it were, like boxes marked "in" and "out." It is more likely, and more in keeping with common sense and modern psychological theory, that the transition from moral to intellectual virtue is developmental; that is to say, a more disciplined intelligence and lively imagination bring about heightened sensibility and help us to realize hidden possibilities of moral character. Though the precise relationship between the two types of virtue seems shrouded in mystery, what we can say with some assurance is that as young people begin to become self-directed they also usually become more emotionally mature and develop greater moral refinement. This is, assuredly, one of the major benefits of a "liberal" education: confrontation with some of the best works of the human mind makes each of us a more complete and "better" person in the sense that we become more aware than we were of our common human nature and the obligations that accompany membership in the human community. Learning can, and does at times, bring about important changes in our disposition to make certain choices. But these changes are impossible to forecast and are non-programmable. Moral virtue, therefore, could never provide a focus for educational theory. The aim of the latter is, and must remain, the attainment of intellectual virtue—or, as Robert Hutchins would have it, making young people "as intelligent as possible." Moral virtue is, for all intents and purposes, unteachable after one leaves early childhood.

This raises an important question in light of the social pressure that currently stresses the attempt to "teach values" and "morality" in institutions of education—including institutions of higher education. What point can there be in, say, requiring undergraduate business majors to take a course in business ethics or medical students to take a seminar in professional ethics? If character is virtually formed and these young people are already disposed to right or wrong actions, what point is there in trying to "teach values"? The answer seems quite clear: there is little point whatever if our goal is to reform character, whereas these subjects can be extremely important ways to *refine* character. Because imagination, intelligence, and will are not discrete entities, the development of intellectual skills clearly also involves the refinement of sensibilities and the heightening of imagination as the student's world becomes larger. But if change is to occur, the avenue through which it will occur late in life is human reason. "Intellectual virtue" is the only plausible objective in formal education. Indeed, it is what the liberal arts, properly understood, have always attempted to help develop.

Through reading literature, for example, the young person lives vicariously and grows in imagination and sensitivity; by studying history, the horizons of that person's experience are extended and his or her sympathies are deepened; by studying philosophy, the student discovers seminal ideas, sharpens analytical skills, and learns the difference between reasonable and unreasonable claims; by studying mathematics, the student learns to respect the authority of sound argument and the persuasive force of proof. The process of education—to the extent that it sharpens intellectual skills, imagination, memory, analysis, and synthesis—can make us better thinkers. To the extent that it deepens our sensibilities, it can take us out of ourselves and increase our awareness of the world of which we are a part. But we cannot expect education suddenly to transform a callous and uncaring person into an Albert Schweitzer or a Mother Teresa.

In a word, a course in business ethics will not make an undergraduate business major an honest employee when he goes to work after graduation. But it will sharpen his analytical skills and make him aware of the subtleties of rationalization and wary of sophistry. If it is well taught, it will help him to appreciate careful argumentation and reasoned judgment and make him suspicious of their opposites. It will not, it cannot, make him a good person. It will not cause him to take pleasure in being honest or courageous, even though it may help him to see which actions are likely to lead to those ends if he finds them pleasurable. By no means are such courses a waste of time; but we delude ourselves if we think they will make our students good people if they are not disposed to be good people long before they enroll in our classes. As Aristotle has shown, what we normally mean by "goodness" has more to do with the sorts of things we take pleasure in than it does with the choices we make to get us to pleasurable ends.

This is not all that can be said on this subject, of course. The student's notion of what is pleasurable can and frequently does change with age. In more mature years, the student will almost certainly discover new arenas within which great treasures are stored and future pleasure might be taken. As I have noted, the movement from moral to intellectual virtue is developmental—intellect, will, and imagination are not discrete entities, and human beings differ from one another in their capacity to grow. Many pleasures previously unknown to a student can be discovered even in the period we call "higher" education, and he may well discover a new range of exciting possibilities and continue to grow and experience new delights. This is one of the great benefits of education. There are pleasures literally too numerous to mention within the worlds of literature, the fine arts, history, mathematics, science, and philosophy. We cannot say with any assurance, however, that in particular cases these pleasures will be ones that dispose a person to perform virtuous actions. For the most part, the latter pleasures are molded into our character long before we enroll in our first college class, engage in dialogue with fellow students, visit museums and galleries, or sit in auditoriums. As a rule, one is not a better person because one now takes pleasure in the writings of James Joyce or the symphonies of Brahms, whereas yesterday one did not. One is better off, perhaps, and more fully developed (certainly more interesting) as a person, but not a bit more honest, trustworthy, or caring. We must be clear about this, because education's supposed failure to make students better people usually results from the failure to distinguish between "reforming" and "refining" young people. The latter is a legitimate goal of education, the former is not.

As a result of liberal studies, we become more fully aware of the consequences of our actions, the range of our influence, and the boundaries of our world. The kinds of things we find pleasurable can change, and this can result in a reorientation of the personality. The "humanizing effect" of studies in the disciplines that make up the liberal arts does, indeed, enrich and elevate our lives. It can make a person aware that the honesty he owes to another he owes to everyone, because obligations are owed to all, not just to some. The liberal arts do invariably enlarge one's world: they deepen sensibilities and expand horizons so that one can see more clearly and vividly what makes up human life and how much alike we all are. This will make a person more sensitive and considerate if he is already disposed to care about others. But if the disposition is not already present, it is doubtful that any profound change can occur. It certainly is not to be expected.

There are a great many lessons to be learned by thinking through Aristotle's argument and adopting his distinction between "moral" and "intellectual" virtue. Some of these lessons have important repercussions for the philosophy of education and for those who would incorporate the teaching of values into our schools. We can reinforce but we cannot "teach" moral values. Moreover, the effort to do so detracts from what the schools can do if they focus their energy on the central purpose of putting young people into possession of their own minds. Autonomous persons are able to make their own decisions about the means most appropriate to desired ends. That is, education—and especially higher education—ought properly to focus on enabling young people to make reasonable, informed choices. But we must be aware that the correctness of the ends toward which those choices are directed is a matter of character, which is formed, for the most part, "in early youth."

For Aristotle, the problem of raising the young was easier than it is for us, because the *polis* played multiple roles in educating young people. That is why Socrates was not worried about leaving his sons in the care of his city after he died. But for us it is a mistake to expect the state or any social institution other than the family and the church to play the role that has always properly belonged to the latter entities. This is especially so given the fact that, when compared with the Athenian city-state, the modern nation-state totters on the brink of moral bankruptcy.

Chapter VIII

DISSENTING OPINION

"We might consider whether a thinking man...would not perhaps do better to make truth and not community his goal, since the latter would indirectly and in the long run be better served by the truth, even bitter truth, than by a train of thought which proposed to serve it at the expense of truth, but actually, by such denial, destroyed from within in the most unnatural way the basis of genuine community."
— Thomas Mann, *Doctor Faustus*

Not everyone in higher education would agree with the arguments advanced in this book. Indeed, there is a growing number of people in higher education who insist that the proper focus of educators at all levels should be on achieving social justice and fostering humane virtues rather than on the seemingly narrow focus of liberating young minds.

I would argue that this is a false dichotomy: social justice cannot be achieved if young people cannot think—and young people will not be taught to think when their professors insist upon thinking for them. It is not enough to try to foster fellow-feeling in open young minds and to pass down the cup of superior wisdom. For who can honestly say that members of our teaching faculties have a sure and certain grasp of the concept of social justice or that, as many argue, cultural diversity will instill in the unwilling fellow-feeling and a sense of community with the rest of the world? These are moot questions and, as long as they remain so, the more necessary it becomes to remain focused on the modest, and defensible, goal of positive freedom.

The academy is full of critics of traditional views of education—from Lillian S. Robinson (who advocates a "female counter-canon") and Henry Louis Gates to Barbara Hernstein Smith and bell hooks (the latter a novelist and critic who insists on using only lowercase letters to spell her name). We met several of these thinkers earlier, particularly in Chapter 4, but one we have not yet encountered is certainly one of the most articulate and persuasive; I speak of Lawrence Levine, professor of history at George Mason University. His book *The Opening of the American Mind*, which attacked the views of Allan Bloom in particular and, *pari passu*, the views expressed here, was both influential and very well received by those on the academic Left. It is deserving of special attention.

In his book, Professor Levine expresses surprise that there are those who are all worked up over the future of higher education in general and the canon in particular. He is well aware that battle lines have been drawn between the preservers of high culture and those with blatantly political agendas. In the midst of what seems to be rampant hysteria, Levine exudes calm. And from the sound of the praise on the book's dust jacket, one gets the feeling that many of his colleagues are relieved that someone, at last, has restored harmony and balance. He gives every appearance of being the still, calm voice of reason in a panic-stricken crowd. But one is reminded that if a person keeps his head when others around him are losing theirs, he probably does not understand the situation. Such is the case, unfortunately, with Lawrence Levine.

At first glance, it would appear that Levine wants to make peace between the warring camps in the battle over control of the canon in higher education. In the end, however, he is less interested in making peace than he is in silencing critics of militant multiculturalism. If one listens carefully, Levine sounds more like an apologist for progress—convinced that all change is for the better—than a bearer of the olive branch. Most of his arguments are designed to rebut critics, but while one must assent to some of Levine's objections, his arguments are largely a reworking of familiar themes. Among other things, Levine argues that: (1) Traditionalists who want to preserve the canon of Western Civilization are merely defending the status quo because they think that all change is inherently threatening; (2) Traditionalists are given to "jeremiads;" they think the sky is falling because they lack any sense of the place of the present struggle in the history of higher education generally; (3) The canon is merely a "repository" in which citizens make deposits and withdrawals. These deposits and withdrawals, furthermore, "are not made in some abstract context of eternal standards and values but in the context of the surrounding culture, its values and needs." That is, determinations about what our students should read are, and always have been, political or ideological, and cannot be made on the basis of the intrinsic worth of the books themselves.

Levine makes some telling points about the reactionary nature of some traditionalist criticism, which admittedly at times sounds a bit hysterical. But, contrary to what Levine and others of his ilk think, there *is* cause for alarm. Though Levine insists that what traditionalists take as signs of a serious breakdown are merely the familiar signs of our continually transforming society, his claims are highly suspect.

To be sure, there never was a Golden Age in higher education when everyone was in agreement about basic curricular requirements. There always were quarrels, sometimes bitter and prolonged, about what students should read—or whether all students should be required to read anything in particular. We know that these quarrels frequently surrounded books that are now regarded as classics, such as Melville's *Moby-Dick*. It is not necessary for Levine to parade the history of higher education before his reader, as he does, in order to demonstrate that older generations of faculty have always had difficulty accepting the ideas of the new. This is well known and

can be said about the tensions between generations going back
at least to ancient Egypt. The fact remains that there is a radical
difference between today's struggles and those in our past.

Militant multiculturalists would have it that the current unrest in our colleges and universities over the canon is nothing
but a quarrel between a bunch of old fogies who want to defend the status quo and their younger colleagues who merely
want to add a few new titles to the reading list. Their views are
perhaps best summed up by Lillian Robinson, who insists that
"no one seems to be proposing—aloud—the elimination of
Moby-Dick or *The Scarlet Letter,* just squeezing them over somewhat to make room for another literary reality, which, joined
with the existing canon, will come closer to telling the (poetic)
truth."[1] It is hardly this simple, or this innocent. On many campuses where the battle lines have been drawn, dialogue between the various camps has all but ceased. In the midst of this
battle stand the undergraduates, unprepared, and totally uninterested—or as Richard Schwartz claims, "We agonize over the
high politics of the school curriculum while students spend
their time playing video games."[2]

What is unique about today's struggles over curricular
change are the claims—stoutly and defiantly maintained by a
growing number of zealots, as by Levine in point #3 above—
that there is simply no way to measure "greatness," that all
values are personal, and that every idea is thinly disguised ide-

ology. In the words of one of Levine's fellow critics, "Literary quality is simply a function of the current interests of the reading public; each public revises the short lists drawn up by publics of the past in accordance with its own cultural needs.... [A] text's acceptance into the canon is and always has been a political decision...."[3] I have sought to cast doubt upon these claims in the preceding pages (and in my last book as well),[4] but, at best, they are moot claims that cannot be taken as true simply because they are asserted to be so. They must be persuasively argued before the gloves come off and the chin thrusts forward.

What is new, then, is that academic decisions are now openly and avowedly made on political grounds at the same time that standards of worth, objective truth, and the possibility of disinterested scholarship have come under fire. What is new is that the burden of proof has shifted from justifying the latest fashion (where it belongs) to justifying what has been long established. In fact, tradition ought to be regarded as, *prima facie*, worthy of being preserved. Increasingly, this is not the case.

The current struggle in American universities is not simply over disagreements about curricular change; it concerns a breakdown in the rules of civilized discourse. Colleagues refuse to listen to one another because each has "the truth," and everyone *else* has been labeled. Everyone has "the truth," of course, because there is no truth, only opinions—and even the dullest sophomore has an opinion. And placing labels on those who disagree with us makes it virtually impossible to resolve differences. In the end, the crisis in our universities and colleges is about values and the denial of objective certainty, and it goes well beyond the walls of academe.

In history, which is Levine's field, fierce quarrels rage over questions of evidence and whether facts are to be replaced by "acceptable (as opposed to warranted) proof." Levine insists that historians have always quarreled about evidence. This is true but also irrelevant, since the question is not what is to count as evidence, but whether or not evidence is to count.

Mary Lefkowitz is much closer to the truth when, echoing Thomas Mann, she notes:

> Because of the confusion about the purpose of the university...we have reached the point where academic discourse is impossible, at least in certain quarters, because the achievement of social goals, such as diversity, has been allowed to transcend the need of valid evidence. But once we accept the idea that instead of truth, there are many truths, or different ethnic truths, we cannot hope to have an intellectual community."[5]

Thus, contrary to what Levine insists is the case, today's problems differ from the curricular struggles of past generations. Despite disagreements, at times quite bitter, academics always held fast to the notion of objective truth and standards of evidence—though they may also have quarreled over which standards to apply.

But today we witness the relativizing of truth based on the privatizing of reality. True has become "true for me" and reality is "the world as I see it." In such a world the individual is infallible, to be sure, but what he knows is of interest to no one else. To abandon the ideal of objective certitude—which admittedly no one can lay claim to with assurance—is to fall back on personal opinion and private hunches. On such a view the most that can be said about a conflicting perception is that it is unlike our own: no better and no worse, only different. This is an absurd view and it is based on the assumption that we can only avoid dogmatism by embracing total relativism: a dangerous and false dichotomy. Champions of such a relativistic view claim to be more tolerant than those who insist upon an objective truth, but their relativism leads in the end precisely to intolerance, since there is no way to reasonably adjudicate differences, no way to resolve moral perplexities morally.

But how is this relevant to our present discussion of the purpose of higher education? To answer this question I need only ask the reader to recall the example in Chapter 5 of citizen Maynard, who sought to do "the right thing," to maintain positive freedom in the face of civil laws. As I argued at that time, the "right thing" is not that action known with certainty to be correct, but that action that seems reasonable to critical intelligence. Rejection of standards of truth and reasonableness render the ideal of positive freedom impossible to achieve. Absolute truth and reasonableness are not attainable by all (or any), but they do function as corrective standards to be approached with hat in hand.

It is ironic that these champions of social justice and humane virtue embrace a relativism that removes all ground from under these concepts and renders human ideals whimsical. In the words of one of their best theorists, Terry Eagleton, relativism leaves its adherents "with no more reason why we should resist fascism [for example] than the feeble pragmatic plea that fascism is not the way we do things in Sussex or Sacramento."[6]

The root cause of these fundamental and seemingly intractable disagreements, as Levine's third point demonstrates, lies with a faulty view of the idea of the university and what it is that universities properly do. The view articulated by Levine, and others, that the university is a mirror that reflects the greater society of which it is a part lacks philosophical grounding: it is descriptive rather than normative. It tells us what universities do, but ignores the question of what they should do. Perhaps Levine is correct when he says that "the American academic world is doing a more thorough and cosmopolitan job of educating a greater diversity of students in a broader and sounder array of courses covering the past and present of the worlds they inhabit than ever before in history."[7] But I am not quite sure what it means to do a "cosmopolitan" job of educating students, and I doubt if it has to do with providing a sound education.

Nor is a sound education to be found in the "tolerance" so heavily praised by Levine and others of like mind. It is well to remember that tolerance is sometimes nothing more than thinly disguised indifference; an open mind may be an empty mind. This is not to say that intolerance is a good thing, but merely to point out that tolerance in itself is insufficient. My students, especially in recent years, may indeed be tolerant, but they are also, as Peter Sacks describes them, "jaded, underachieving, highly demanding, yet lacking any respect for standards of excellence." These students "view themselves as consumers who intend to study just a handful of hours a week for all their classes, and who expect, as a minimum, a solid B grade for their efforts."[8]

Judging from recent data regarding "grade inflation," this is just what they are receiving. And this is in large part because of the views advanced by Charles William Eliot, president of Harvard toward the end of the nineteenth century, who insisted that "the university must accommodate itself promptly to significant changes in the character of the people for whom it exists." This is untenable; the university cannot possibly hope to be a "faithful mirror" to the heterogeneous mix it aims to educate. Properly conceived, it is not a supermarket established in order to cater to the whims of a fickle public. The university does not have many purposes, as some critics have maintained; it has one central purpose. To discover this purpose, the university must focus attention on the distinctive role it can play in a democratic society, and, as we have seen, this means putting young people into possession of their own minds. This is not a description of what is being done at present; it is a prescription for what ought to be done if our young people are to achieve real freedom and our democratic society is to flourish.

The response of critics to traditionalist criticism is symptomatic of the failure of the university itself. It ignores a problem because it does not perceive anything worth defending. High culture is simply one culture among many; values are in flux; and there is no vision of the university's mission that extends beyond the merely pragmatic. The university does not view itself, and it is not viewed by such postmodern spokesmen as Levine, as an institution that has any specific purpose. It is simply a place where students go to accumulate credits and to become "cosmopolitan," whatever that may mean.

Contrariwise, as Robert Hutchins once said, the university is not a mirror, it is a beacon. It does not exist to satisfy wants, it exists to satisfy needs—human needs that are not specific to individuals or to particular cultures. And the greatest human need is to become intellectually free.

Chapter IX

WHERE DO WE GO FROM HERE?

"The hope is that the embers do not die soon."—Allan Bloom

Like anyone else who has been teaching for more than thirty years, I look back with a sense of nostalgia on "the good old days." I will almost certainly go to my grave convinced that the present generation has it all wrong. But, as I suggested in the last chapter, I know things were never all that good in higher education. I have done the research and read the proper books; I have listened carefully at keyholes and kept a watchful eye. Things have always been pretty confused, and educators have always fought their petty battles and tried to avoid facing fundamental issues. At the risk of being labeled what Richard Hofstadter called a "paranoid spokesman," however, I would insist that the situation has never been as bad as it is at present. We seem to be farther than ever from the goal of the liberally educated citizen.

This is not to deny that there are remarkable successes in academia, but only to insist that these successes are more by accident than by design. To be sure, there are bright college students who are eager to learn and willing to challenge themselves in order to get as much as possible from a liberating college experience. There are dedicated individuals and groups of faculty who are committed to teaching and learning: English professors who still love literature, historians who respect evidence and continue to search for truth about our past, philosophers who practice the Socratic method, social scientists who can see beyond statistics, and natural scientists who want their students to enlarge their perspective and balance their love of mathematics and science with deepened sensibilities. And there are administrators who are not merely business people or politicians whose sole directive is efficiency and the bottom line.

Thus, despite the twisted and aimless path our institutions of higher learning have taken, there are occasional signs of hope along the way. But these signs are a meager return for the immense amount of effort and money spent on the enterprise. So much time is wasted, so much energy is lost, so many opportunities are squandered in the typical four-year undergraduate college. Our experiment with higher education, on balance, must be regarded as one of the great disappointments of the twentieth century.

Accordingly, certain things must take place if we are ever to set things right. The consequences of not facing up to this need for substantial reform are more serious now than they ever have been, because the young people who are graduating from our institutions of higher learning face problems that dwarf those encountered by prior generations. If these college graduates cannot use their minds, then they (and we) are in serious trouble. I have attempted in this book to suggest how we might recall the purpose of education; now I would like to turn to specific remedies that would go at least part way toward achieving that purpose. In doing so, I shall begin with an area that might at first seem tangential to our main concern: intercollegiate athletics.

The main problem with intercollegiate athletics is not so much that the football coach at a major university makes considerably more money than the president, or, worse yet, than a tenured full professor who might be a Nobel laureate, but that intercollegiate athletics as pursued at the highest levels on many American campuses has little or nothing to do with the true purpose of education.

Consider some particulars. Athletic "scholarships" at the University of Colorado, where athletes participate in a dozen varsity sports (fewer than many Division I schools), recently totaled $1,117,000.[1] In response to pressures from advocates of Title IX, the NCAA reports that universities are now adding new sports especially for women, such as archery, badminton, bowling, equestrian, ice hockey, squash, synchronized swimming, team handball, and water polo. One must surely ask, what has this to do with educating young minds?

The standard defense that athletics teach "cooperation, leadership, competitiveness, and responsibility," that they "build character," is doubtless sound, but it cannot be used to defend *intercollegiate* athletics at the Division I level, specifically. Among other things, it flies in the face of the fact that only 1 percent to 2 percent of the students at major state universities participate in intercollegiate athletics and graduation rates among males in "revenue sports" such as basketball and football are as low as 29 percent.[2] Further, one must raise ethical questions about the exploitation of many of these athletes who are recruited to play sports, given special rewards, encouraged to take a mindless course load (with majors in such subjects as "General Studies"), and allowed to drop out along the way. Indeed, at the University of Tennessee, Linda Bensel-Meyers, a professor of English, was recently pilloried for revealing that twenty-two football players were enrolled in fluff courses that do not lead to any degree whatever. In response to questions by a reporter from the *Kansas City Star,* she noted that "...instead of offering athletic scholarships to give underprivileged students access to education, UT has implemented a system that exploits athletes for institutional profit, replacing affirmative-action opportunities with a system of institutionalized slavery."[3]

Clearly, there is a problem. The question is what, if anything, can be done about it? I have several suggestions, and I hasten to add that I am no enemy of college athletics, having coached intercollegiate tennis successfully for more than fifteen years, and being one of the millions who spend the weekend glued to the television set watching whatever sports happen to come on. But there is something rotten in the athletic department and drastic measures are in order.

When he was president of the University of Chicago, Robert Hutchins cut the funding for intercollegiate athletics altogether. It was not a popular move, but it made a statement and was an attempt to reestablish priorities at a prestigious university. I would not follow Hutchins's lead, though I would take some steps that many will regard as equally drastic.

To begin with, I would collapse the distinction between Division II and Division III programs and eliminate athletic "scholarships" completely. These scholarships are a major expense and the source of much that is wrong in intercollegiate sports. The arguments that are employed to defend them are bogus. If there is a genuine student need for financial assistance and cultural diversity, as is usually alleged, it is not self-evident that both ends cannot be achieved by other means —especially if the athletic scholarship money is made available to all students on the basis of need and academic ability.

At the Division I level, where problems abound, I would recommend eliminating all pretense by admitting that major sports at that level are a proving ground for professional athletics—especially football, basketball (both men's and women's), and, to a lesser extent, baseball. Young people who choose to participate in athletics at that level should not be required to attend classes and they should be paid to play, the teams at the major universities becoming minor league teams sponsored by the universities and their alumni. It is difficult to imagine that students or alumni really care if the athletes they pay to see also spend some of their time in the classroom.

In the event that one or more of the athletes on these teams actually wants to pursue an education, they can pay tuition along with everyone else. We would hope in our democratic society that all citizens would want an education. But for some the urge comes later than for others, if it comes at all. In any event, these people will be better able to attend college with the money they make from athletics. This step would remove the hypocrisy and pretense that exist at present and the universities would be able to apply the most promising of current business practices to organized sports in order to deal with current deficits. In the event that the costs of fielding a professional team become prohibitive, the universities can simply choose to move to the Division II level where financial losses from athletics are typically less than at the Division I level—and would be even less so without athletic "scholarships." In the event that costs remain prohibitive, the universities would have to eliminate some of the sports programs—a reasonable proposal given the large number of sports that involve such a small number of students (and one that is already being adopted by a growing number of Division I schools). Dropping football at a typical Division II school that currently offers scholarships to athletes, for example, can save that school close to $200,000 a year, according to a recent NCAA study.

The beauty of this model lies in its honesty, since very few of the athletes in major sports at the Division I level are students in anything but the loosest sense of that term. Or, to strike a more positive note, the perks that athletes receive at the Division I level, such things as scholarships, certain meals, medical treatment, laundry, clothes, and housing, "do not come close to representing the value of the athletes to the school in terms of publicity, winning revenues, and additional donations"; this model would acknowledge that these athletes are professionals and treat them accordingly.

Stephanie Pare, the author of the comments just quoted, does not propose steps nearly as radical as mine. She thinks it will suffice to

change our perspective on college sports and develop a model
of sport as other than a forum where certain parties can make
money and student-athletes can strive for fame. Rather than
yielding to commodification and focusing on the results and
pressuring teams to win, our universities, coaches, and
student-athletes should focus on process-oriented version of
sport that recognizes that sport is a social phenomenon that
produces social relationships among participants."[4]

I think these recommendations are sound, but they do not
go far enough. What Pare hopes to see cannot happen as long
as athletics are regarded as somehow academically defensible
and, at the same time, a business. As things stand at present, the
tail does, indeed, wag the dog.

The model I have suggested takes us to the heart of the
problem, since it allows professional athletes to be recognized
and rewarded for what they are and eliminates the need for
watchdog organizations such as the NCAA to scurry about the
halls of academe looking for possible violations of bogus codes
that merely disguise the fact that so many athletes under review want nothing more than simply to play for pay. At the
Division II level in my model, where costs are not so prohibitive and profits not so grand (in most cases), there is hope that
athletes can compete for the love of their sport. If not, then
there is the intramural level. Such an ideal would bring us
closer to the balance proposed by Pare and which the Greeks

sought when they advocated "gymnastics" as a part of every young man's education.

This point brings us back to the main topic at issue, which is the nature and purpose of the academy as an educational institution. What specific curricular proposals might turn higher education around and redirect it toward its proper goal?

To begin with, high schools must be held accountable for the quality of student they certify as ready for college. The data suggest that the average high school graduate reads at the eighth grade level and is purblind without a calculator. He or she knows nothing of world history and very little about modern science or current events. It is folly to expect these young people to be able to read actively, think critically, solve problems, and acquire enough information about their world to become enlightened citizens. As far as the institutions themselves are concerned, the current preoccupation with "difference" and the belief in computer technology as an answer to all our educational prayers are misguided, and they exact a great cost—financially as well as educationally.

In addition to pushing for higher standards in the secondary schools and resisting the temptation to siphon off resources that are barely adequate to serve the purpose for which the academy exists, there are a number of specific steps that would help to restore a sense of purpose. I hinted at some of these steps at the end of the first chapter. Here I will expand and elaborate.

The certification and accreditation programs that are mandated by external agencies and sometimes tend to overwhelm undergraduate education need to be carefully monitored and in some cases be dismantled. Aside from practice teaching, for example, I am unaware of any concrete benefits resulting from teacher certification programs. If there are any, they must be weighed against the immense costs. These programs have brought about a mammoth bureaucracy, mountains of jargon, a preoccupation with means, and a host of requirements that discourage bright students and threaten to stifle their education. In one instance that I am aware of, state requirements have resulted in the reduction of elective credits for students seeking certification to one credit *in four years.* This is patently absurd. Our private high schools, some of them the elite schools of this nation, do not require teacher certification and yet manage to turn out exceptional students who do well in higher education and beyond.

There are practical reasons why institutions of higher education feel bound to purchase acceptance with outside agencies, of course. But as a matter of principle, the imposition of strictures by groups of narrow specialists outside the academy is clearly antithetical to the purpose of a liberal education. If accreditation by these agencies cannot be avoided, the requirements should be added at the end of the completion of the baccalaureate degree and should not be allowed to encroach on what is of first importance.

The problem lies not only with external agencies, however. Within the academy itself, far too much emphasis is placed on major requirements, without asking what these requirements have to do with the purpose of undergraduate education. It is not clear, for example, what the proper relationship is between positive human freedom and, say, a major in business administration, computer science, chemistry, philosophy, electrical engineering, or theater arts. In some cases the relationship seems remote, at best, but it is highly doubtful that a major, *any major,* can realize the goals of liberal education by itself. Louis Menand was quite possibly correct in saying that "the undergraduate major seems to me an institution that is at best pedagogically inefficient...and at worst a contributor to the perpetuation of a fundamentally arbitrary definition of knowledge."[5] At the very least, there should be guarantees that major programs be held to reasonable limits to allow for a balance among electives, major courses, and general "core" courses at the undergraduate level. Such a balance would appear to be a necessary condition for realizing the goals of a liberal education—the sufficient condition being the proper selection of those courses.

Because general education is at the heart of what is left of the liberal arts in American academies of higher learning, at least one-third of the undergraduate load should be reserved for those studies. Ideally, this preserve would focus on the Great Books of Eastern and Western civilization. This would include some of the classics from the history of science and it would be supplemented by at least one foreign language, basic mathematics (through the calculus), and at least one year of laboratory science. It is astonishing that in our advanced society there are still putatively educated people who cannot comprehend or write a paragraph, who insist that creationism is a scientific theory, or who have never heard of Heisenberg's uncertainty principle.

Major requirements should be held to one-third of the undergraduate load as well. If it is deemed necessary to extend this load, the additional hours should be added at the end of the four years of the student's "normal" undergraduate experience, as with accreditation. At present, major requirements are allowed to cut into both general courses and electives. This is indefensible. Despite the fact that the study of one subject area is a valuable tool for acquiring the intellectual discipline necessary for real thought, it is not clear that this should be regarded as an open invitation to add major courses endlessly, as is often the case. Just how much study in one academic area is necessary will vary from discipline to discipline, but in no case should it be allowed to reduce the number of electives or general courses (see Appendix A).

Electives are the bastard offspring of the modern elective system that started at Harvard in 1883. No one seems to know quite what to do with them: there seems to be no rhyme or reason why students take the electives they do take, and faculty members generally regard electives as academic residue. In many cases, faculty members will simply urge students to take more major courses. Students, on the other hand, seem to prefer courses that are "useful" and will not threaten to lower their GPAs. Bear in mind that an American Council of Education survey recently revealed that the main goal of 78 percent of the undergraduates surveyed was "to get a better job."[6] Clearly, some attempt should be made to render the electives coherent and defensible from an educational point of view.

Accordingly, it would be appropriate for the faculty to draw up a list of recommended elective courses that would not be career-oriented, but would help to realize the student's overall need to become an educated person. Further, students should not be allowed to take elective courses in their major field(s) of study. Finally, if all of the elective courses were graded on an optional grading system, it would alleviate students' anxiety about their GPAs (see Appendix B).

What principles, though, should guide these discussions and give them focus? It is one thing to say, as I have, that academic subjects should "put young people into possession of their own minds," but since all who teach would insist that their courses do precisely that, consensus will be slow in coming. What is necessary for the faculty involved is to focus attention on the question of which courses *outside their own disciplines* they would acknowledge to be necessary for a liberal education. That is, what sorts of courses are necessary for young people to learn to master their own language and the languages of mathematics and science? What academic subjects will better enable students to develop their active imaginations and improve their thinking, speaking, writing, calculating, listening, and problem-solving skills? What subject matter do they need to know in order to direct attention away from the here and now to the anticipated future and to become informed citizens of the world in the twenty-first century?

Some answers to these questions seem clear; others are harder to come by. If we consult the data available to see which academic subjects generally refine the skills mentioned in the list above, we find that students who major in English, foreign language, economics, philosophy, government, anthropology, biology, mathematics, chemistry, physics, accounting, finance, and engineering tend to score above the mean on national tests, such as LSAT, MCAT, and GRE tests.[7]

I am not a great believer in test scores, and they prove nothing, strictly speaking. They may simply indicate that these subject areas attract the sharper minds to begin with. But the data accord with the intuitions of many of those involved in higher education that these are the "tougher" academic areas and are therefore more likely to develop vital intellectual skills. Taken together with courses in world literature and the fine arts to help develop the imagination, these courses are a likely place to start when working up lists of recommended electives. In addition, students of the new century will need to know history if they are to become informed citizens of the world. This is especially so for Americans, who are notoriously ignorant of history in general and their own history in particular.

If then, in addition to reading the Great Books, students were required to study mathematics, basic English, at least one year of a foreign language, natural science, and the "recommended electives" made up of courses in the above academic areas, arranged in clusters with every attempt made to order and integrate disciplines wherever possible, they would be well served indeed (see Appendix C). Much would depend on the success of the advising process, which I shall discuss presently.

In the event that students feel that they have need to take a course or courses not on the list of recommended electives, those students could petition their advisor to allow them to make a substitution. This petition would be in written form and would be followed by a conference with the advisor in which the student seeks to persuade the advisor that the course(s) in question more nearly accords with his or her educational goals and, more importantly, the goals of a liberal education. The value of such conferences to both students and faculty members would be immeasurable.

To make it possible for faculty members to take the time necessary to hold such conferences, and to provide good academic advice generally, academic advising must be made an institutional priority. Further, members of the faculty must be convinced that these duties are as important as teaching. This means, of course, that advising must be rewarded with recognition, release time, and/or remuneration. The faculty's mentoring role comes to the fore in the advising situation more than anywhere else, and this is where the opportunity arises to help the student achieve the level of sophistication necessary to make informed choices about courses—whether or not these courses will get them a better job. As things now stand, with rare exceptions, advising is an afterthought; students seldom even attend advising sessions, and many members of the faculty regard it as a chore.

Another step toward halting the tendency of majors to become inordinately large, and to protect students from proselytizing major advisors, would be to require that students in their first two years work with academic advisors in disciplines *outside* their major field. Indeed, educational goals would be more nearly realized if students were not allowed to declare a major at all until their junior year. In this regard, we should keep in mind what Louis Menand is anxious to remind us about, namely, that "majors" are of relatively recent origin: "...before the 1880s no one imagined that history, political science, economics, anthropology, and sociology constituted distinct areas of study."[8] In any event, assistance from nonmajor advisors would be a step in the right direction. If there are technical questions advisors need to ask about unfamiliar disciplines, they can phone a colleague in that discipline. In the end, the student is victimized by even the most well-meaning and sincere faculty advisor who regards his or her discipline as the only one worthy of serious consideration. Those of us who have done time in academies of higher learning know how all of us mark out our territory and fight to protect it.

In general, the issue of advisement in colleges and universities that allow students to take elective courses should be addressed in conjunction with the question of purpose. It is absurd on the face of it to simply hand nineteen-year-old college sophomores a class schedule and ask them to choose courses, willy-nilly, that will further the goals of a liberal education. If students are to make *informed* choices among electives, they must already know what those courses attempt to teach; but if this were true, they would not need to take those courses in the first place! Faculty responsibility in the education of young people, we should recall, is to certify that the

baccalaureate degree their institution confers upon their recommendation is a mark of a process that has been completed
to their professional satisfaction: the person who graduates is
presumably an educated person, or well on the way to becoming one. In this regard, faculty advisement in the realm of elective courses is of central importance, certainly as important as
the selection of "core" courses and the determination of major
requirements.

These are items of major concern, but several other items
suggest themselves as ways to restore a sense of purpose to the
academy:

(1) We need to stress the need for articulating in a coherent fashion the inter-relatedness of general courses. These
courses should not merely be introductory courses to recruit
academic majors. One way to do this could be to arrange
courses in "clusters" of three or four taught by faculty in different departments on a common theme. An example might be a
cluster on "creativity" taught by faculty in art, literature, psychology, and philosophy. Another might be a cluster on "the
origins of American democracy," taught by faculty in history,
political science, and government. Or a cluster on "human nature," with courses in biology, anthropology, and psychology.
Focusing on the relationship that ought to exist among such
courses will force faculty members to come to grips with philo-

sophical issues about the nature and purpose of education, which may open some lines of communication and increase awareness among members of faculties that disciplines other than their own also have strengths (see Appendix C).

(2) We should reward teachers for becoming involved in planning and teaching general courses through incentive pay or released time from teaching. This would have the added benefit of drawing the institution's best teachers into the general education pool. In keeping with this, I would add:

(3) While continued research and publication are important ways for faculty members to keep abreast of ideas in their field of expertise and to keep their minds alive, the pressure to "publish or perish" at the undergraduate level should be reduced. Tenure and promotion should not be tied to publication in narrow, professional journals; it should be tied directly to success in the classroom, which can be measured more reliably than most critics would like to admit. The other dimension of this precept is to reward good teaching of core courses as well as courses within specific disciplines with pay increases and institutional recognition.

We must hope that at the level of what is now euphemistically called "post-secondary" education, faculty somehow gain a broader perspective on their own role in education proper. They must come to see their discipline in relation to others that are equally important and begin to think about the place of their discipline in the context of liberal education. Quarrels over territory are pointless; the "culture wars" are a waste of precious energy and of no real benefit to our students—even if they are invited to participate, as Gerald Graff recently suggested.

Finally, in order to open up lines of communication among faculty and help to bring an end to the war of words, colleges and universities might integrate departmental offices geographically. If offices share corridor and building space, the people who occupy those offices might begin to talk to one another.

At the institutional level, administrators must support teaching, which is the soul of education. They must not buy into prevalent myths about education as job training, spend precious revenue on athletic programs that cater to the few, fall for the latest technical gimmick, or modify curricula to suit the latest trend. Disciplines that do not "pay their way" may nonetheless be central to the liberal arts, and these programs must be protected against erosion arising from momentary lack of student interest. If these programs are important, then they must be "sold" to the students, not abandoned as fiscally burdensome.

The name of the game these days, however, is "R and R"— recruitment and retention. Institutions scramble to give students what they want with little concern for what they need. This is a dangerous game, and one in which the students are victimized without knowing it. In the day-camp atmosphere that colleges and universities carefully foster for them, students get caught up in tailgating and tail-getting, grudgingly go to classes, and at the end of four or five years receive a piece of paper that tells them they are educated. Those institutions that play the game successfully will survive, but the students who pass through the halls will not approach any closer the goal of human freedom. The students lose out, of course, but society also suffers, because those students cannot possibly function as free citizens of an increasingly complicated world.

Everyone in higher education has a stake in a common enterprise, which is to free young people from stupidity, prejudice, and parochialism, and to enable them to think for themselves. It is precisely this sort of freedom that empowers human beings, regardless of color or gender. And until, or unless, we turn our attention to the question of how best to achieve that goal, we will continue to cheat our students and fool ourselves.

Appendix A

Suggested Four-Year Undergraduate Program

This plan is quite close to the division of major credits, core requirements, and electives into thirds recommended in the text. It is a bit heavy in the core requirements—forty-nine—but those could be modified depending on the student's level of preparation coming into college.

Freshman Year (32 Semester Credits)

Basic English 3+3*

Mathematics (College Algebra and Analytic Geometry) 3+3*

Laboratory Science (Physics, Chemistry, or Biology) 4+4

Great Books 3+3

Recommended Electives 3+3

Sophomore Year (32 Semester Credits)

Mathematics (Calculus) 3+3

Foreign Language 4+4

Great Books 3+3

Recommended Electives 6+6

Junior Year (32 Semester Credits)

Major Credits 9+9

Recommended Electives 6+6

Miscellaneous 1+1

Senior Year (32 Semester Credits)

Major Credits 12+15

Senior Seminar (Great Books) 3+0

Miscellaneous 1+1

* These areas can be bypassed or adapted by students who bring with them especially strong backgrounds in basic English and mathematics.

Appendix B

RECOMMENDED ELECTIVE CREDITS

(Specific courses to be selected by faculty outside the discipline upon recommendations from those within that discipline)

Note that these elective courses are to be *guaranteed* to the students. Any additions to major requirements (such as accreditation, ancillary requirements, or a second major) would have to be added to the total and not allowed to encroach on these electives. These courses should be offered with a credit/non-credit option to alleviate fears of reducing students' GPAs.

Fine Arts
Philosophy
Literature
Speech

Government

Economics

Psychology

Sociology

History

Anthropology

Accounting (for non-business majors)

Finance (as above)

The principle behind the recommended electives is that students would select them with an advisor's help. The electives would be selected to fill in gaps in the student's background and would not be in the student's major field of interest.

Appendix C

CLUSTER COURSES

Clusters might be arranged in the following fashion. Students would be encouraged to take two or three courses in each cluster, and the clusters would be arranged around a theme.

Example #1: "Human Nature"

Monday

9:00 AM	Biology
10:00 AM	Anthropology
11:00 AM	Psychology

Wednesday

9:00 AM	Biology
10:00 AM	Anthropology
11:00 AM	Psychology

Friday

9:00 AM   Common Session

Example #2: "Power"

Monday

9:00 AM   Literature

10:00 AM   History

11:00 AM   Sociology

Wednesday

9:00 AM   Literature

10:00 AM   History

11:00 AM   Sociology

Friday

9:00 AM   Common Session

A successful adaptation of the cluster concept is in use at Southwest State University (Marshall, Minnesota), which adds a "voyage" to the clusters at the end of each semester. The trip lasts a week or ten days and involves visits to geographical regions germane to the cluster theme. "Voyages" have been to such places as Toronto, Paris, London, Vietnam, and Central and South America.

Notes

Preface

1. Allan Bloom, *The Closing of the American Mind* (New York: Simon and Schuster, 1987), 380.

2. Ibid., 370.

Chapter I: *The Purpose of Higher Education*

1. Scott Buchanan, *Embers of the World* (Santa Barbara, Calif.: Center Occasional Paper, 1970), 64.

2. Brand Blanshard, *Four Reasonable Men* (Middletown, Conn.: Wesleyan University Press, 1984), 247.

3. Paul Vitz, *Psychology as Religion: The Cult of Self-Worship* (Grand Rapids, Mich.: William B. Eerdmans, 1977), 52.

4. Donald Campbell, as quoted in Vitz, 46.

5. Vitz, 15 ff.

6. *Chronicle of Higher Education,* May 1990.

7. Jacques Ellul, *The Technological Society,* trans. J. Wilkinson (New York: Vintage Books, 1964), 78.

8. Michael Polanyi, *Personal Knowledge* (Chicago: University of Chicago Press, 1984), 216.

9. A. Bloom, 340.

10. This may seem a bit of an overstatement, and corroborating data are admittedly hard to find. Some evidence does exist, however, in the wide usage of anthologies in undergraduate education. The popularity of books that contain highly specialized articles from professional journals raises serious questions about their appropriateness at the undergraduate level and the motivation that leads to their selection in the first place. As suggested here, the problem seems to me to be a part of a larger, cultural problem, which I have termed "inverted consciousness." See my essay, "Our Hatred of Values," *Modern Age* (Summer 1985): 242-249. I plan to explore the phenomenon of inverted consciousness more fully in my next book, *Lost Piety: The Self as God*.

11. Gabriel Marcel, *Man against Mass Society* (Chicago: Gateway Press, 1969), 59.

12. Carnegie Commission on Higher Education (San Francisco: Jossey-Bass, 1973).

13. The term multiculturalism, or its cognate "cultural pluralism," may actually be something of a misnomer as currently used. In philosophy, for example, the term chiefly refers to feminism, since in the ten-year period between 1986 and 1996 there were ten times the number of publications dealing with feminist issues as with racist issues, "and more than all areas of non-Western philosophy combined," according to Daniel Bonevac. This led him to conclude that "[I]ndeed, one would not go far wrong in saying that multiculturalism in philosophy has mostly meant feminism" ("Manifestations of Illiberalism in

Philosophy," *Academic Questions* 12, no. 1: 17). In general, this movement, in its more militant mode, is cause for alarm among those who care about the restoration of purpose to the academy. For extended comment, see my book *Rediscovering Values: Coming to Terms With Postmodernism* (New York: M.E. Sharpe, 1997).

Chapter II: *Debunking Some Myths*

1. *Southwestern Peach*, 4 December 2000, 47.
2. Baruch Spinoza, *The Chief Works of Spinoza,* trans. R. Elwes (New York: Dover, 1951), IV, Prop. LXVII.
3. George Panichas, *The Critical Legacy of Irving Babbitt* (Wilmington, Del.: ISI Books, 1999), 59.
4. John Henry Newman, *The Idea of a University* (New Haven: Yale University Press, 1996), 19.
5. Mark Van Doren, *Liberal Education* (Boston: Beacon Press, 1959), 62.
6. Matthew Arnold, *Culture and Anarchy* (New Haven: Yale University Press, 1994), 10.
7. Carl Sagan and Ann Druyan, *Shadows of Forgotten Ancestors* (New York: Random House, 1992), Chapter 19.
8. Jacob Burckhardt, *The Civilization of the Renaissance in Italy* (New York: Harper and Row, 1958), 143.

Chapter III: *Education or Indoctrination?*

1. See, for example, Carol Gilligan, "Why Should a Woman Be More Like a Man?" in *The Pleasures of Psychology,* eds. D. Goleman and D. Heller (New York: New American Library, 1986), 40-51.
2. John Locke, *Second Treatise on Government* (New York: Prometheus

Books, 1986), 63.

3. John Stuart Mill, *On Liberty* (New York: W. W. Norton, 1975), 77.

4. Van Doren, 62.

5. Richard Posner, *Law and Literature* (Cambridge, Mass.: Harvard University Press, 1994), 282.

6. Ibid., 317.

7. Hershel Parker, *Flawed Texts and Verbal Icons* (Evanston, Ill.: Northwestern University Press, 1984), 137.

8. Oscar Wilde, *The Artist as Critic* (New York: Random House, 1969).

9. Charles Dickens, *The Old Curiosity Shop* (London: Chapman and Hall, 1867), 173.

10. Harold Bloom, *The Western Canon* (New York: Riverhead Books, 1994), 302.

11. Posner, 19.

12. H. Bloom, 34.

13. Martha Nussbaum, "Invisibility and Recognition: Sophocles' *Philoctetus* and Ellison's *Invisible Man,*" *Philosophy and Literature* 23, no. 2 (October 1999): 272.

Chapter IV: *How Not to Read a Book*

1. Chinua Achebe, "An Image of Africa," in *Chant of Saints: A Gathering of Afro-American Literature, Art and Scholarship.* (Urbana: University of Illinois Press, 1979), 319, 321. In a later version of this paper—reprinted in *Hopes and Impediments* (New York: Doubleday, 1989)—Achebe refers to Conrad as a "thorough going" racist.

2. Richard Rorty, *Consequences of Pragmatism (Essays 1972-1980)* (Minneapolis: University of Minnesota Press, 1982), 152.

3. Posner, 182 ff.

4. Stewart Wilcox, "Conrad's 'Complicated Presentations' of Symbolic Imagery," in the Norton Critical Edition of *Heart of Darkness,* 2nd ed. (New York: W. W. Norton, 1971), 191. Wilcox has convincingly shown that Marlow's repeated references to Brussels as a "white sepulchre" has its sources in Matthew 23:27–28, where Christ is venting his anger at the Pharisees, who "are like unto whited sepulchres, which indeed appear beautiful outward, but are within full of dead men's bones, and of all uncleanness." As Wilcox notes, "In the strongest language he ever used, Christ reproved [the Christians] for the false righteousness that covered their inward wickedness." Not only is Brussels a "white sepulchre," but the ivory is gleamingly white, as are the skulls that adorn Kurtz's fence posts. In the novel, to be sure, the hypocrisy of the Europeans is readily apparent and the simplistic white=good, black=evil dichotomy is knocked off its foundations.

5. Joseph Conrad, *Heart of Darkness,* 69.

6. From "Geography and Some Explorers," quoted in the Norton Critical Edition of *Heart of Darkness,* 118.

7. Conrad, 7. Note also Marlow's criticism of "the philanthropic pretense of the whole concern,...their talk...their government...their show of work" ("their" refers to the Europeans), 25.

8. Ibid., 50.

9. Ibid., 37.

10. Ibid., 52.

11. Ibid., 42.

12. Ibid. Regarding Kurtz's lack of restraint, see pp. 52 and 58.

13. David Lodge, "O Ye Laurels," *New York Review of Books,* August 8, 1996, 16.

Chapter V: *Citizenship in a World of Difference*

1. Anne Wortham, "Errors of the Afrocentrists," *Academic Questions* 5 (fall 1992): 36. Wortham claims that this type of multiculturalism, which she calls "corporate pluralism," has an essentially "conservative aim, [which] is to use the political system to recover historical groups and reinforce traditional communities." She contrasts this with what she calls "individualist pluralism," which "envisions the United States as a unified nation composed of many individuals of diverse beliefs, interests, group affiliations, and cultural backgrounds.... [It] holds that individuals ought to be free, within the limits of respect for the rights of others, to adopt the values, philosophies, religions, or practices of any culture they wish" (36). The former is inconsistent with the notion of citizenship I defend in this chapter; the latter is not, by any means.

2. Scott Buchanan, *So Reason Can Rule* (New York: Farrar, Strauss, and Giroux, 1982), 139.

3. Chaim Perelman, *The New Rhetoric,* trans. J. Wilkinson and P. Weaver (Notre Dame, Ind.: University of Notre Dame Press, 1969), 31.

4. This is one of the few lines in *Social Contract* that reflects Rousseau's Romanticism. For the most part, this particular book is unusual and might have been written by any Enlightenment thinker— as evidenced by its impact on Kant. Generally, I would agree with Babbitt that Rousseau's Romanticism is pernicious and one-sided to a fault (see his *Rousseau and Romanticism*).

5. Buchanan, *So Reason Can Rule,* 139.

6. Alexis de Tocqueville, *Democracy in America* (New York: Alfred Knopf, 1945), vol. II, 2.

7. Lisa Newton, ed., *Taking Sides* (New York: Dushkin, 1998), 72.

8. Wortham, 37.

9. Kitaro Nishida, *An Inquiry into the Good,* trans. M. Abe and C. Ives (New Haven: Yale University Press, 1990), 144. Nishida also embraces a view of positive freedom essentially like the one advanced in this book. He notes, "True freedom is the necessary freedom of functioning from the internal character of the self" (163).

Chapter VI: *The Liberal Arts and the Public College*

1. Plato, *The Republic*, trans. F. Cornford (Oxford: Oxford University Press, 1965), 286.

2. Richard Weigle, "Report of the President," *Bulletin of St. John's College* XX, no. 3 (1968).

3. Robert Hutchins, *The Learning Society* (New York: Mentor Books, 1968), 112.

4. Ibid., 115.

5. Jerome Bruner, *The Process of Education* (Cambridge: Harvard University Press, 1960), 33.

6. Ibid., 33.

7. Alvin Kernan, ed., *What's Happened to the Humanities?* (Princeton: Princeton University Press, 1997), Appendix, 245-258.

8. Ibid.

9. Ibid., 215.

10. A. Bloom, 353.

11. Buchanan, *So Reason Can Rule,* 139.

12. Unfortunately, recent data collected by the National Association of Scholars (*N. A. S. Update* 10, no. 4) suggest that English departments in twenty-five of the most prestigious small colleges in America are dancing to the postmodern melody. All but four of the departments polled have "abandoned require

ments for core English and American literature surveys." Only two of these prestigious colleges require that their English majors take a course in Shakespeare. Further, in most of these institutions, where "culture critique rather than literary study has become the principle theme of many departments," emphasis on major authors generally has been replaced by a concern for feminist and minority literature. Clearly, there is room for concern here, as faculties in the English departments at these institutions apparently find it difficult to address complex issues of quality in a heated political atmosphere where black-and-white thinking holds sway. This does not bode well.

Chapter VIII: *Dissenting Opinion*

1. David Richter, ed., *Falling into Theory* (Boston: Bedford Books, 1994), 157.

2. Richard Schwartz, *After the Death of Literature* (Carbondale, Ill.: Southern Illinois University Press, 1997), 35.

3. Richter, 112.

4. Curtler, *Rediscovering Values: Coming to Terms with Postmodernism* (New York: M. E. Sharpe, 1997).

5. See her *Not Out of Africa* (New York: HarperCollins, 1996), 173.

6. Terry Eagleton, *Illusions of Postmodernism* (Oxford: Blackwell, 1996), 28.

7. Lawrence Levine, *The Opening of the American Mind* (Boston: Beacon Press, 1996), 17.

8. Peter Sacks, *Generation X Goes to College* (Chicago: Open Court, 1996).

Chapter IX: *Where Do We Go from Here?*

1. NCAA Annual Report, www.ncaa.org, 1999.

2. Ibid.

3. *Kansas City Star,* 25 June 2000; C-16.

4. Stephanie Pare, "Playing College Sports," (N.Y.U. Law School, Internet, 1998).

5. Richter, 95.

6. Ibid., 89.

7. Educational Resources Information Center. In *Proceedings and Addresses of the American Philosophical Association* 62, no. 5 (1989), 854.

8. Richter, 95.

Bibliography

Achebe, Chinua. "An Image of Africa." In *Chant of Saints: A Gathering of Afro-American Literature, Art and Scholarship,* edited by Michael Harper and Robert Stepto. Urbana, Ill.: University of Illinois Press, 1979.

————. *Hopes and Impediments.* New York: Doubleday, 1989.

Aristotle. *Nichomachean Ethics.* Translated by Martin Ostwald. Indianapolis: Bobbs Merrill, 1962.

Arnold, Matthew. *Culture and Anarchy.* New Haven: Yale University Press, 1994.

Babbitt, Irving. *Rousseau and Romanticism.* New York: Transaction, 1991.

Berlin, Isaiah. *Four Essays on Liberty.* New York: Oxford University Press, 1970.

Blanshard, Brand. *Four Reasonable Men.* Middletown, Conn.: Wesleyan University Press, 1984.

Bloom, Allan. *The Closing of the American Mind.* New York: Simon and Schuster, 1987.

Bloom, Harold. *The Western Canon*. New York: Riverhead Books, 1994.

Bonevac, Daniel. "Manifestations of Illiberalism in Philosophy." *Academic Questions* 12, no. 1: 14-22.

Bruner, Jerome. *The Process of Education*. Cambridge, Mass.: Harvard University Press, 1960.

Buchanan, Scott. *Embers of the World*. Santa Barbara, Calif.: Center Occasional Paper, 1970.

———. *So Reason Can Rule*. New York: Farrar, Strauss, and Giroux, 1982.

Burckhardt, Jacob. *The Civilization of the Renaissance In Italy*. New York: Harper and Row, 1958.

Carnegie Commision on Higher Education. San Francisco: Jossey-Bass, 1973.

Chronicle of Higher Education, May 1990.

Conrad, Joseph. *Heart of Darkness*. 2nd ed. New York: W. W. Norton, 1971.

Curtler, Hugh Mercer. "Our Hatred of Values." *Modern Age* (Summer 1985): 242-249.

———. *Rediscovering Values: Coming to Terms with Postmodernism*. New York: M. E. Sharpe, 1997.

Dickens, Charles. *The Old Curiosity Shop*. London: Chapman and Hall, 1867.

Eagleton, Terry. *Illusions of Postmodernism*. Oxford: Blackwell, 1996.

Educational Resources Information Center. In *Proceedings and Addresses of the American Philosophical Association* 62, no. 5: 839-854.

Ellul, Jacques. *The Technological Society*. Translated by John

Wilkinson. New York: Vintage Books, 1964.

Gilligan, Carol. "Why Should a Woman Be More Like a Man?" In *The Pleasures of Psychology,* edited by D. Goleman and D. Heller, 40-51. New York: New American Library, 1986.

Heller, Erich. *The Disinherited Mind.* New York: Meridian Books, 1965.

Hutchins, Robert. *The Learning Society.* New York: Mentor Books, 1968.

Janus. "Januarian Manifesto." *The Gallatin Review* (Winter 1993): 141-173.

Kansas City Star, Section C, 25 June 2000.

Kernan, Alvin, ed. *What's Happened to the Humanities?* Princeton: Princeton University Press, 1997.

Larvis, John. "Why a Proper Core Curriculum Is Political and Ought Not to Be Politicized." *Intercollegiate Review* 28, no. 2: 24-32.

Lefkowitz, Mary. *Not Out of Africa.* New York: HarperCollins, 1996.

Levine, Lawrence. *The Opening of the American Mind.* Boston: Beacon Press, 1996.

Locke, John. *Second Treatise on Civil Government.* New York: Prometheus Books, 1986.

Marcel, Gabriel. *Man against Mass Society.* Chicago: Gateway Press, 1969.

Mann, Thomas. *Doctor Faustus.* Translated by H.T. Lowe-Porter. New York: Alfred Knopf, Inc., 1948.

Mill, John Stuart. *On Liberty.* New York: W. W. Norton, 1975.

National Association of Scholars Update 10, no. 4.

NCAA Annual Report, www.ncaa.org, 1999.

Newman, John Henry. *The Idea of a University.* New Haven: Yale University Press, 1996.

Newton, Lisa, ed. *Taking Sides.* New York: Dushkin, 1998.

New York Review of Books, 8 August, 1966.

Nishida, Kitaro. *An Inquiry into the Good.* Translated by M. Abe and C. Ives. New Haven, Conn.: Yale University, 1990.

Nussbaum, Martha. "Invisibility and Recognition: Sophocles' *Philoctetus* and Ellison's *Invisible Man.*" *Philosophy and Literature* 23, no. 2 (October 1999): 257-283.

Pare, Stephanie. "Playing College Sports." N. Y. U. Law School (Internet), 1998.

Parker, Hershel. *Flawed Texts and Verbal Icons.* Evanston, Ill.: Northwestern University Press, 1984.

Perelman, Chaim. *The New Rhetoric.* Translated by J. Wilkinson and P. Weaver. Notre Dame, Ind.: University of Notre Dame Press, 1969.

Peters, R. S. *Ethics and Education.* Atlanta, Ga.: Scott, Foresman, 1967.

Plato. *The Republic.* Translated by F. Cornford. Oxford: Oxford University Press, 1965.

Polanyi, Michael. *Personal Knowledge.* Chicago: University of Chicago Press, 1962.

Posner, Richard. *Law and Literature.* Cambridge, Mass.: Harvard University Press, 1994.

Reeves, Thomas. *The Empty Church.* New York: Free Press, 1996.

Richter, David, ed. *Falling into Theory.* Boston: Bedford Books, 1994.

Rorty, Richard. *Consequences of Pragmatism (Essays 1972-1980).* Minneapolis: University of Minnesota Press, 1982.

Rousseau, Jean Jacques. *Social Contract.* Translated by W. Kendall. Chicago: Gateway Press, 1954.

Sacks, Peter. *Generation X Goes to College.* Chicago: Open Court, 1996.

Sagan, Carl, and Ann Druyan. *Shadows of Forgotten Ancestors.* New York: Random House, 1992.

Scholes, Robert. *The Rise and Fall of English as a Discipline.* New Haven, Conn.: Yale University Press, 1998.

Schwartz, Richard. *After the Death of Literature.* Carbondale, Ill.: Southern Illinois University Press, 1997.

Spinoza, Baruch. *The Chief Works of Spinoza.* Translated by R. Elwes. New York: Dover, 1951.

Tocqueville, Alexis de. *Democracy in America.* New York: Alfred Knopf, 1945.

Van Doren, Mark. *Liberal Education.* Boston: Beacon Press, 1959.

Vitz, Paul. *Psychology as Religion: The Cult of Self-Worship.* Grand Rapids, Mich.: William B. Eerdmans, 1977.

Wilcox, Stewart. "Conrad's 'Complicated Presentations' of Symbolic Imagery." In *Heart of Darkness.* 2nd ed. New York: W. W. Norton, 1971.

Wilde, Oscar. *The Artist as Critic.* New York: Random House, 1969.

Wortham, Anne. "Errors of the Afrocentrists." *Academic Questions* 5 (Fall 1992): 36-50.

Index